FIND AND USE YOUR INNER POWER

FIND AND USE YOUR INNER POWER

EMMET FOX

HarperSanFrancisco
A Division of HarperCollins*Publishers*

FIRST HARPERCOLLINS PAPERBACK EDITION PUBLISHED IN 1992.

Library of Congress Cataloging-in-Publication Data
Fox, Emmet.
        Find and use your inner power / Emmet Fox. — 1st
HarperCollins pbk. ed.
            p.   cm.
        ISBN 0-06-250407-X
        1. New Thought.   I. Fox, Emmet.   II. Title.
BF639.F6719—1991
248.4'8998—dc20   91-55083
                                                                        CIP

---

04 05 06   RRD   30 29 28 27 26 25 24 23

To
all men and women everywhere
who believe that the will of God
for man
is
freedom, health, and harmony
and that
these things can be attained by
learning the laws of life and
applying them

KNOWLEDGE IS POWER

Contents

CONTENTS

Preface

The Laws of Thought are the Laws of Destiny. *Whatever you believe with feeling, that you bring into your life.*

These little essays are intended to instruct the reader in Basic Spiritual Truth and to furnish material for short meditations. They were published once a week over a number of years.

The subjects are usually handled in a light and amusing style and often deal with familiar incidents in everyday life. The reason for this policy is as follows:

The writer has always believed that fundamental Spiritual, Philosophical, and Metaphysical Truths could be stated in the plainest and simplest language, so that any intelligent child could understand them. It is true that most writings on these great subjects have been very obscure and full of technical jargon, but the present writer believes that to be unnecessary.

Certain subjects, such as the higher mathematics, for instance, must remain out of reach of the layman, but this is not important because they do not concern his practical life. The understanding of Spiritual Truth, on the other hand, is not only the concern of Everyman but is a vital need of his life, and it must necessarily therefore be possible for him to obtain it in a form that he can use. The loftiest and the most profound spiritual knowledge alike must be capable of being understood by any reasonably intelligent person over ten years of age.

These great Truths are actually revealed to us, not in the pages of inaccessible treatises, but in the seemingly petty and unimportant details of everyday life. Such practical details—the problems and experiences of day to day living—present the questions and also furnish the answers to the great problems of human life, when one has the Spiritual Key.

The writer tries as far as possible to avoid the use of technical terminology, and never employs a word of three syllables where a word of two syllables will do.

Each of these Sparks illustrates one or more of the Laws of psychology or metaphysics. Try in each case to find out for yourself which is the particular Law involved, and then see if you are using that Law constructively in your own life. If you are not, you must change your habits of thinking without delay, for *the Laws of Thought are the Laws of Destiny*.

A SMALL SPARK CAN START A GREAT FIRE

FIND AND USE YOUR INNER POWER

Take It Easy

on't hurry. You are going to live for-ever—somewhere. In fact, you are in eternity now; so why rush?

Don't worry. What will this thing matter in twenty years' time? You belong to God, and God is Love; so why fret?

Don't condemn. As you cannot get under the other fellow's skin, you cannot possibly know what difficulties he has had to meet—how much temptation, or misunderstanding, or stupidity within himself he has had to overcome. You are not perfect yourself and might be much worse in his shoes. Judge not!

Don't resent. If wrong has been done, the Great Law will surely take care of it. Rise up in consciousness and set both yourself and the delinquent free. Forgiveness is the strongest medicine.

Don't grumble. Consume your own smoke. Your own concept is what you see; so treat and change that.

Don't grab. You cannot hold what does not belong to you by right of consciousness anyway. Grabbing postpones your good.

Don't shove. You are always in your right place at the moment. If you don't like it, change it scientifically by rising in consciousness. This will be permanent.

Cafeteria

Don't wait for something to turn up. Don't be content to let things drift along, hoping for the best. It is not spiritual to "put up" with inharmonious conditions. If the conditions of your life are not to your liking, you must get to work on your own consciousness and, by raising that above the outer picture, cause those conditions to become something nearer to your heart's desire. And you must keep on doing this until you find your True Place.

I had an amusing experience when I first came to America. Passing an attractive looking restaurant, I went inside, and, selecting a table, sat down and waited. Strangely, as it seemed to me then, nothing happened. I sat there and continued to wait—indefinitely as it seemed. I could not understand the reason for this neglect. All around me, people were enjoying their food, and only I was left out in the cold. After a while the truth of the situation slowly dawned on me—it was a cafeteria. (This system had not yet made its appearance in England in those days.)

I then quickly realized that while there was plenty of food of every kind to be obtained, one had to go forward and claim it for oneself, or go without.

The universe is run exactly on the lines of a cafeteria. Unless you claim—mentally–what you want, you may sit and wait forever. Of course, you should not claim in detail—that is outlining—but you must positively claim health, harmony, and True Place, if you really want those things.

Worm Gets Ideas

To me the butterfly teaches the most wonderful and the most important lesson that we human beings ever have to learn. You all know his story. He is a beautiful butterfly now, but he was not always a butterfly. No, indeed. He began life, and he lived what seemed to him a very, very long time, as a worm—and not a very important kind of worm either—what we call the humble caterpillar.

Now the life of a caterpillar is a sadly restricted one, in fact, it could be taken as the very type and symbol of restriction. He lives on a green leaf in the forest, and that is about all he knows.

Then one day something happens. The little caterpillar finds certain strange stirrings going on within himself. The old green leaf, for some reason, no longer seems sufficient. He begins to feel dissatisfied. He becomes moody and discontented, but—and this is the vital point—it is a *divine discontent*. He does not just grumble and complain to the other caterpillars, saying "nature is all wrong." "I hate this life." "I can never be anything but a worm." "I wish that I had never been born." No, he is discontented, but it is a *divine discontent*. He feels the need for a bigger, finer, and more interesting life. His instinct tells him that where there is true desire there must be fulfillment, because "where there's a will, there's a way."

And so the wonderful thing happens. Gradually the worm disappears, and the butterfly emerges, beautiful, graceful, *now endowed with wings*—and instead of crawling about on a restricted leaf, he soars right above the

3

trees, right above the forest itself—free, unrestricted, free to go where he likes, and see the world, and bask in the sun, and, in fact, be his own True Self—the free and wonderful thing that God intended him to be.

Now this wonderful story is intended to be the story of every human soul. It is up to you to develop your wings by the scientific use of creative imagination so that you may fly away to your heart's desire.

An All-In Policy

What has your religion done for you? For years probably, you have been attending church, reading spiritual books, studying the Bible, and so forth. Now I suggest that you have a spiritual stock-taking. Ask yourself—what has your religion done for you? What difference has it made in your life, in your home, in your affairs? How much peace of mind has it given you? How much courage? How much understanding? How much opportunity for service? For, make no mistake, real religion does give all these things.

If your spiritual stock-taking does not turn out to be satisfactory, if your religion is not working in this way— if on examining your life you find there are a number of places at which you are not demonstrating, if certain needs are still lacking to you, if there are still negative things that refuse to go—I believe that you will find the explanation to lie in the following law: *What you put into your religion, that you get out of it.*

If you put 5 percent of yourself and your life into your religion, you will receive a 5 percent dividend or demonstration. If you put 20 percent of yourself and your life into your religion, you will receive a 20 percent demonstration. And until you put 100 percent of yourself and your life into your religion you will not receive a 100 percent demonstration.

A complete, all round demonstration calls for an *all in* policy.

Saluting the Christ in Him

W e often hear the expression "saluting the Christ in him," or "seeing the Christ in him," and we may well ask ourselves what that phrase really means. Well, it is simply the practical application of the rule of Jesus Christ, "Judge not according to appearances but judge righteous judgment."

Each one of us has a Divine Self that is spiritual and perfect but that is never seen on this plane. That is the true man, God's man, and is what we call today, "the Christ within." It is the *real* you, or the *real* him or her.

Now whenever you dwell upon or realize the presence of the Christ within—within yourself or within anyone else—outer appearances begin at once to improve, and both the amount of the improvement and the rate at which it takes place, will depend on the number of times that the Indwelling Christ is "saluted" or realized, and the degree of realization attained.

This saluting of the Christ need take only a moment, and it never fails to benefit the individual concerned and the person who does it also.

When someone seems to be behaving badly, or when you hear bad news concerning him, salute the Christ in him instead of accepting the appearance. When a given condition seems to be inharmonious, whether it be an organ of the body, a business arrangement, or anything else, see God working in it—better still, *"Golden Key"* it—and this saluting of the Christ will heal it.

If somebody displeases you, silently salute the Christ in him, and say aloud whatever seems best. If someone says:

"John Smith is sick," salute the Christ in Smith (know that in reality he is spiritual and perfect) and refuse to accept the negative statement. If someone says something against John Smith's character, salute the Christ in him, refuse to discuss the matter, and of course do not repeat it.

The more often you salute the Christ in others, the sooner you will find it in yourself.

Stand By for Quarantine!

When you are praying or treating about a particular thing, you should handle it, mentally, very carefully indeed. The ideal way is not to think about it at all except when you are actually praying about it. To think about it in between, especially to talk to other people about it, is exceedingly likely to invite failure.

When a new problem presents itself to you, you should immediately know the Truth about it, and then decline to consider it except in the light of Truth. I call this "putting a subject in quarantine," and whenever I have been able to "quarantine" a problem of my own I have always demonstrated very easily and very well.

Even an old, long-standing problem can be "put in quarantine" today, if you mean business and will resolutely break the habit of constantly thinking over that problem.

Everyone knows that a photographer must not expose unfixed film to daylight if he wants to get results. Everyone knows how careful a chemist is to isolate (i.e., "quarantine") his materials in the laboratory, since the slightest contamination of one chemical by another will probably ruin any experiment. What many Truth students do not seem to understand is that mental operations have to be just as carefully safeguarded if demonstrations are to be made.

Whenever you think about any subject, you are treating it with your thought—either for good or evil.

The Will of God

The most wonderful thing in the world is the Will of God. The Will of God for you at the present moment is something glorious and beautiful, thrillingly interesting and joyous, and, in fact, far beyond anything that you could possibly sit down and wish for with your conscious mind.

It is unfortunate that so many people seem to assume as a matter of course that the Will of God for them is likely to be something dull or burdensome, if not positively repulsive.

"I suppose it is God's will for me, so I must put up with it," people say when talking about some condition that they hate. "Thy will be done," pious people say in the face of death or tragedy. All this is absolutely wrong. The Will of God for man is life, health, happiness, and true self-expression, and it is only in connection with these things that we can say, "Thy will be done."

Trouble or suffering of any kind does not come from God. It is an indication that there is a lesson to be learned by us, and the trouble itself furnishes us with the very opportunity that we need in order to learn that lesson, so that such a thing need never happen to us again.

Trouble is valuable opportunity. Experience is priceless instruction. The Will of God for you is always something joyous and fine.

*Spreading the Truth**

To convey the knowledge of the Truth to others has always been considered one of the most effective means for one's own spiritual development. In the ancient schools of Wisdom it was an accepted duty regarded as binding upon all. Jesus himself has said to us: "Go ye therefore and teach all nations," and, "This gospel must first be preached to all the world."

In this age when practically everyone can read and write, the circulation of inexpensive booklets and pamphlets is one of the most effective ways of spreading the Truth. A written statement is impersonal. It raises no arguments. It is never inopportune, because the recipient will naturally wait until he is ready before reading it. It can be gone over several times at leisure if it is not readily understood at first contact.

You cannot do a more useful thing for your fellow man, and for yourself too, than to put in somebody else's way any one of the Truth books that have helped you personally. This practice, in Shakespeare's phrase, "is twice blessed. It blesseth him that gives and him that takes."

Hear a modern parable:

John Smith bought a Truth book. He handed it or mailed it to his friend, Mr. Brown, whom he knew to be going through a difficult time. Brown was immensely struck with it—these ideas were quite new to him—he

---

*See Fifteen Points in *Power Through Constructive Thinking*.

carried the little book about in his pocket, followed the instruction given, and made a beautiful demonstration. He was so enthusiastic that he broached the subject to a business colleague, Jones, during lunch, presented him with his own copy, and wrote off for a fresh supply for himself that night.

Jones, as it happened, was not really interested. He took the little book merely out of politeness, glanced at the first page, and threw it away. He was about to tear it across as was his custom when discarding documents, but the attractive cover restrained him and he put it aside uninjured.

His stenographer, Miss Robinson, found it among the litter, and, liking the look of it, took it home and studied it carefully. She determined to try it on a personal problem that was making her own life miserable at the time, and being unusually simple and direct in her methods, demonstrated within three days. She then mailed her copy to her brother in a distant city. For years he had been hungry for a living religion, and, briefly, the booklet changed his life. Naturally he himself went on to spread the Truth in his own way, as did each of the others in the chain.

In this parable, we see that John Smith, by a single act, became the means of blessing quite a number of people (most of whom he never heard of), and that the good results of that first act went on indefinitely.

Until the people learn the Truth, it cannot set them free.

The Dove

In prayer or treatment it is the thought, and not the words used, that matters. The words are merely an indication of the thought. Some people find that the right idea develops more easily when a good many words are used, and of course such people should use as many words as they feel the need of. Others are embarrassed by the difficulty of finding many words, and in that case two or three phrases are quite sufficient. A well-known man was healed of consumption using only the single statement "God is Love." Of course, he dwelt upon it intelligently until he thoroughly realized something of what those words must mean.

We all remember the story of Ali Baba and the cave. Unless one knew the exact word it was impossible to open the door. The thought might be the precise one required, but unless the exact word *sesame* was uttered, the door remained obstinately shut. Barley? Wheat? Grain?— No use. *Sesame* was the magic word, and nothing else whatever would do. Now in treatment it is the exact opposite of this. Not the word, but the thought in mind is what counts. As long as the thought is right we may use any language that we find helpful. Our treatments are prayers and not incantations.

Often it is well to dispense with words altogether, as getting in the way, and introducing a dangerous moment of delay. When God visits His people, it is their business to welcome Him immediately and to experience Him, not to try to form intellectual definitions. We must never keep God waiting. Directly the realization, which is

Emmanuel,* presents itself, you may have to drop all words—cease "working" there and then, and *possess* it. If you postpone this for ever so short a time you will find, when you come to look for it, that the Dove has flown away again, and you will have to wait until he returns. And that *may* be quite a long time.

People sometimes say "I will give half an hour to this case," or it may be "I will go through the Seven Main Aspects of God." Excellent things to do, but if it should happen that after three minutes, or when you have finished the second Aspect, *the Dove alights,* then receive him instantly with open arms. To think, "I will finish my treatment first," is to turn him away. This feeling of the real Presence of God is itself, of course, the perfect treatment; the end to which all our statements are but means.

He saw the heavens opened and the Spirit like a dove descending upon him (Mark 1:10).

*Matthew 1:23.

Satan Gets Away With It

G od is the only Presence and the only Power. God is the only Cause, and His will is completely fulfilled at every moment. What we call evil or error is a false belief that we form about good. It has no power apart from the power we give it by believing in it.

This is the Truth teaching, but it happens too often in practice that the student, instead of really getting rid of the conventional belief in the reality of evil, merely changes the name of his devil and goes on recognizing him under some new alias.

It is the standard practice with swindlers each time they are exposed, promptly to change the name of the firm and then restart the old fraud under the new style. When once the name of "John Smith" has appeared in the police reports, he does not, unless he is a very negligent villain indeed, again solicit your confidence under that title. It would be waste of time. What he does is just buy a new brass plate and start up the old racket again as "Messrs. Brown & Jones" or whatnot. Later, when this in turn is exploded, he once more changes the style of the firm to, let us say, "Robinson & Company," and so on *ad infinitum*. And he never lacks victims, because so long as people will allow themselves to be swayed by mere names, instead of examining the underlying thought, they have no protection.

This is just the way in which apparent evil acts. Satan, having been thoroughly exposed as the Devil, with horns, hoofs, and tail, promptly alters his name and address, and goes on tempting those who should know better into sin, sickness, and death, by giving himself some new description such as error, mortal mind, hypnotism, time, climate, heredity, and so forth. And only too often he gets away with it quite successfully. Instead of being emancipated from fear, his victims are now ten times more under its dominion than ever they were in their orthodox days, and they suffer accordingly. They have merely changed the label on their superstition.

As long as you recognize the reality of anything but God, under any pretense, you are harboring fear, and you will punish yourself inevitably. It makes no difference whether you choose to give your bogey the name of Satan, Old Nick, Mephisto, or to call it climate, or heredity, or age, or anything else.

I am the Lord, and there is none else, there is no God beside me (Isaiah 45:5).

The Bible Unveiled

T he Bible is too often looked upon as an out-of-date and rather dull compendium of conventional religion of the sanctimonious type. There could not be, however, a greater mistake. Those who find it dull are those who have had it presented to them in the wrong way. Read in the light of the Spiritual Interpretation, it will be found to be a practical textbook of thrilling interest, containing, as it does, clear explanations and definite guidance for any and every difficulty that can arise in everyday life.

Religious difficulties, the healing of the body, the poverty problem, home or business worries, are all dealt with and provided for in the Bible.

You Are a Mental Being

Man is a mental being, and to know this is the first step on the road to freedom and prosperity, for as long as you believe yourself to be primarily physical, a superior kind of animal, you will remain in bondage—in bondage, that is to say, to your own habits of thought, for there is no other bondage. Mind is primary, but mind must have embodiment, and the embodiment of your mind is found in your visible conditions—the kind of health you have, your financial position, your business connections, the sort of home you have, and all the thousand and one things that make up your present environment.

This being the case, you will see how foolish it is for you to endeavor, as do most people, to improve your conditions by altering your environment while leaving your mind unchanged. To attempt this is to attempt the impossible and to foredoom yourself to failure and disappointment. Mind is cause, and experience is effect; and so, as long as your mind remains unchanged, it will continue to produce just those effects or experiences of which you are anxious to be rid. If you do not like the experience or effect that you are getting, the obvious remedy is to alter the cause and then the effect will naturally alter too.

God's Hour

G od's hour is the most important event in the day. It may consist of thirty minutes or longer, according to the need of the individual, but it should hardly be less than that if you really mean business in your spiritual life.

God's hour is the time in which you read the Bible or other spiritual books and meditate and pray.

The practical secret of health, happiness, and prosperity, and of constant spiritual growth is to make God's hour the principal, that is to say, the most important event in your day. Let that be the center line, as it were, about which all other activities revolve. Let anything else be postponed or omitted rather than that God's hour should be neglected. Let any other engagement be canceled in favor of this. Let any other work go undone rather than this should be missed.

God's hour need not be held at the same time every day although it will be helpful if this can be done. The essential thing is that God's hour be the most important event in the twenty-four hours, and that everything else be secondary to that.

Millennium

As the Truth of the Omnipresence and Availability of God seeps more and more into people's minds, vast changes for the better will come over the human race. These changes, in the beginning at least, may be accompanied by a certain amount of confusion and apprehension, but that stage will not last very long.

First of all poverty will disappear—this change will begin in the English-speaking countries, then it will be seen in Continental Europe, and later among the other civilizations. This means the end of slums with their unholy trinity of poverty, hunger, and dirt. All will have true prosperity without victimizing one section of the community on behalf of another. Of course, this will mean the end of crime as well.

Next, sickness and disease will go. People will demonstrate healthy bodies as a matter of course, and live, in full activity, to an advanced age.

So rapidly will the human consciousness improve that the thousand-and-one fears, jealousies, grudges, resentments, and so forth, that spoil people's lives today, will be absolutely a thing of the past, and war itself will cease to exist—war between nations, and industrial war too.

Think of a world with no armies and no navies, no police departments, no prisons, no hospitals, no poor houses, no orphanages, no locks on doors or drawers or banks or safe deposit vaults, because there is no need for such things.

Think of this new world, and help it to come to birth by believing in it, expecting it, and praying for it.

19

Spotlights

od is not interested in your past history, but in what you are *now.* Now is the day of salvation.

You are healthy because you are happy not happy because you are healthy. A healthy body grows out of a happy mind.

If you have no time for prayer and meditation, you will have lots of time for sickness and trouble.

Where you stand today does not matter; it is the direction in which you are moving, and the rate at which you travel, that count.

The biggest fool of all is the man who bothers about outer things and neglects his own spiritual development.

The only depression that you can meet is the depression thought in your own consciousness.

You really do not know John Smith; you only know the idea that you form of John Smith.

Cause and Effect

W hatever you experience in your life is really but the outpicturing of your own thoughts and beliefs. Now, you can change these thoughts and beliefs, and then the outer picture must change too. The outer picture cannot change until you change your thought. Your real heartfelt conviction is what you outpicture or demonstrate, not your mere pious opinions or formal assents.

Convictions cannot be adopted arbitrarily just because you want a healing. They are built up by the thoughts you think and the feelings you entertain day after day as you go through life. So, it is *your habitual mental conduct* that weaves the pattern of your destiny for you, and is not this just as it should be?

So no one else can keep you out of your kingdom— or put you into it either.

The story of your life is really the story of the relations between yourself and God.

Studying the Bible

For the spiritual study of the Bible, by far the best edition to use is the ordinary King James version. Have a Bible with type large enough to be read with comfort. A dollar or two extra spent on your Bible is worthwhile since you do not buy one every day.

As a general rule, it is not well to work through the Bible steadily from end to end, but rather to select any portion as you feel led at the time. Whichever section interests you most at the moment is usually likely to be best for you at that time. Read the Bible in the light of the spiritual interpretation, using the principal keys and symbols, noting the meanings of proper names, and so forth, as you come to them.

The Bible will usually give you a special message for yourself, fitting your need at the moment. In order to get this, you should claim frequently while you are reading: *"Divine Intelligence is inspiring me."*

Do not go to the Bible to get confirmation for your own ideas but rather to be taught something new.

"Speak Lord, for Thy servant heareth."

Symptoms and Causes

I f you have made many efforts, as you probably have, to set things right, but without any real success, the reason is to be found just here: You have been tampering with symptoms and leaving your mind, the real cause of the trouble, untouched. You have been wrestling with circumstances, with people, and with things, and leaving your mind unchanged; and it is just that mind of yours that is causing all the trouble, all the time, and will continue to do so as long as it remains in its present state. You have been struggling to transform yourself by renewing your conditions, whereas the Law is that we are transformed by the renewing of our minds.

If you want perfect health, if you want abundant prosperity, happiness, a good home, congenial friends, beauty, joy, and thrilling interest in your life, you can have them, if you really want them. But you must want them enough to take trouble enough to find out the only way to get them. You must want them enough to take the trouble to learn how to think, since *thought is the only cause.*

The Cup and the Lip

A n experience that comes to many people may be described as follows: In business life or in their personal affairs they frequently find themselves starting some desirable project and carrying it on without much difficulty up to the threshold of completion, whereupon, for some unknown reason it seems to jam tightly. The last step or the last two steps just cannot be taken. Seemingly everything is ready to ensure success, and then at the eleventh hour, the door closes.

And this experience occurs not once but time after time in one project after another. An important sale is all but completed; all parties concerned seem to be satisfied; but when the moment for signing the contract comes, the sale falls through. Or an important position is all but secured; satisfactory interviews take place; and then at the last moment, someone else is appointed. Or an important meeting is arranged, with a great deal of pains, between two people, and at the last minute the most unexpected happening prevents their meeting. And so on.

These I call "cup and lip" cases since they illustrate so well the old proverb, "There's many a slip 'twixt the cup and the lip." Such a run of misfortune can be broken by realizing: "I belong to God. My work is God's work for God works through me. God's work cannot be hindered or delayed. Of course, God always finishes successfully whatever He begins. God's work must go through to completion. My work is His work, so it reaches full fruition. I thank God for this."

How to Meditate Easily

Truth students are constantly urged to practice meditation on Divine things and, indeed, there is no more powerful form of prayer. It is the Practice of the Presence of God in its most effective form, and is the quickest way out of sin, sickness, and inharmony. But, unfortunately, many people have a fixed idea that they cannot meditate. "I am not spiritual enough," they say, or "I have had no mental training along that line," and so they cut themselves off from the quickest form of spiritual growth. Now, the fact is that everyone can and does meditate. Even the most seemingly material people constantly meditate—only they do not meditate on Divine things.

Thousands of men meditate deeply upon the subject of baseball during the season, without in the least realizing that they are doing so. What usually happens is something like this—John Smith gets up in the morning and immediately picks up all the problems of life where he left them before going to sleep. He goes down to breakfast and engages in conversation about family matters, domestic problems, and so forth. On the railroad platform he buys a paper, reads the headings on the front page, and becomes involved in national and foreign politics or the latest crime. Then the train comes in and, having selected a seat, he turns over to the baseball page. Here he reads steadily for ten or fifteen minutes, and now a change takes place. Gradually, as he reads about the ball games and becomes absorbed in what he is reading, all other subjects fade out of his mind. Home troubles, business troubles, politics, crime, all are forgotten. Presently he lays down the paper and becomes lost in the contemplation of his subject. He thinks about prominent players. He criticizes the management of his own favorite team. Possibly he thinks of certain changes that he would like to see made in the rules of the game—and much more along the same line. The next thing he knows, thirty or forty minutes have passed, and he has arrived at his destination.

Now, here is an excellent example of a first class meditation—except that it has been about baseball instead of about Divine things. This man read up his subject for ten or fifteen minutes and thus got away from the general stream of thought. Having done this, he proceeded to think through and about his subject until he became absorbed in it—his technique was perfect.

Now if you will imitate him, except that you will read a spiritual book for ten or fifteen minutes, and then think about God—taking perhaps the Seven Main Aspects in turn—think about your spiritual self, think about the Truth of Being in any shape or form, you will have made a wonderful meditation too. And if you do this you cannot fail of remarkable results.

Sentiment Slays

Sentiment is usually a short cut to unhappiness and failure. It is more deadly than poison gas, more cruel than the Inquisition, more subtle than self-love.

Sentiment really means pretending. It means making believe that an emotion that is really dead is still alive. It means pretending that something is fine or joyous or worthwhile, when in fact it is none of these things. Thus it means a waste of time, a waste of the soul substance that is lavished upon a lie. Worst of all, sentiment shuts us off from the realization of good in the present moment.

Sentiment usually pretends that some happiness is lost beyond recall, or else it persuades us to worship an unreal abstraction of some kind on the ground that actual conditions are not worth caring about.

Live in the present and let the dead past bury its dead. No good thing that ever existed is out of reach when you understand the spiritual nature of Being. See to it that today and tomorrow are filled with beauty and joy, and this you can do through Treatment. Remember that people never sentimentalize over *present good;* they enjoy it, and thereby glorify God. When they sentimentalize, it is always for something supposedly out of reach.

No good experience is out of your reach because God Himself is with you.

Bear Hugs Kettle

I once read an anecdote of the Far West that carries a wonderful metaphysical lesson. It appears that a party of hunters, being called away from their camp by a sudden alarm, left the camp fire unattended, with a kettle of water boiling on it.

Presently an old bear crept out of the woods, attracted by the fire, and, seeing the kettle with its lid dancing about on top, promptly seized it. Naturally it burnt and scalded him badly; but instead of dropping it instantly, he proceeded to hug it tightly—this being Mr. Bruin's only idea of defense. Of course, the tighter he hugged it the more it burnt him, and of course the more it burnt him the tighter he hugged it, and so on in a vicious circle, to the undoing of the bear.

This illustrates perfectly the way in which many people amplify their difficulties. They hug them to their bosoms by constantly rehearsing them to themselves and others, and by continually dwelling upon them in every possible manner, instead of dropping them once and for all so the wound would have a chance to heal.

Whenever you catch yourself thinking about your grievances, say to yourself sternly: "Bear hugs kettle," and think about God instead. You will be surprised how quickly some long-standing wounds will disappear under this treatment.

Thought Is Destiny

Y ou think, and your thoughts materialize as experience, and thus it is, all unknown to yourself as a rule, that you are actually weaving the pattern of your own destiny, here and now, by the way in which you allow yourself to think, day by day and all day long.

It is altogether in your own hands. Nobody but yourself can keep you down. Nobody else can involve you in difficulty or limitation. Neither parents, nor wives, nor husbands, nor employers, nor neighbors, nor poverty, nor ignorance, nor any power whatever can keep you out of your own when once you have learned how to think.

The Science of Living is the Science of Thought.

Don't Be a Tragedy Queen

When things go seriously wrong there is a strong temptation to cast oneself for a tragic role, to feel deeply injured and even embittered. The result of this, however, is only to make it more difficult to get things right again. Indeed, it may be quite impossible to demonstrate at all so long as this attitude lasts.

Self pity, by making us feel sorry for ourselves, seems to provide an escape from responsibility, but it is a fatal drug nevertheless. It confuses the feelings, blinds the reason, and puts us at the mercy of outer conditions.

In the old-fashioned dramas a favorite role was the Tragedy Queen. It was traditional for her to stalk about the stage in heavy black with an intolerable air of injured innocence. She never made any attempt to put things right, and she invariably came to a sad end.

Don't be a tragedy queen—whether you are a man or a woman, for it is not a question of gender but of mental outlook. No matter what happens, refuse to take it tragically. Absolutely repudiate a crown of martyrdom. If you cannot laugh at yourself (which is the best medicine of all), at least try to handle the difficulty in an objective way, as though it concerned somebody else. To be tragic is to accept defeat. To refuse to be tragic is to affirm victory. Know that you can be victorious and insist upon victory. Realize: *God in me is stronger than anything I have to meet.*

Fundamental Truth

The principal revelation of the Jesus Christ Teaching is the Omnipresence and Availability of God and the belief that because God not only transcends His universe but is everywhere immanent in it—that He indwells in it— it must in reality reflect His perfection. It is prayer that opens the door of the soul so that the Divine Power may work its will to harmony and peace.

This religion teaches that physical ailments are really maladies of the soul outpictured on the body, and that with the healing of the soul accomplished, the healing of the body must follow. The soul is vivified by drawing closer to God through prayer and meditation, and by changing one's outer conduct to bring it more completely in harmony with God's law.

It teaches the efficacy of Scientific Prayer to reshape one's whole life for health, harmony, and spiritual development. By Scientific Prayer we mean the Practice of the Presence of God.

Register Joy and Hold It

I f you really believe in the existence of God you should be happy and cheerful. Even if conditions for the time being are difficult or repugnant, you should understand that such things can only be a temporary picture. God has all power, and God is good; so life must be good too. Once you know this, it can only be a matter of time before you will demonstrate both health and happiness.

Meet the world with a smile. You owe this to God, to fellow man, and, above all, to yourself. If you go about with a face like an east wind, what can you possibly expect to attract from the world?

When I say smile, of course, I mean a real smile, not an artificial one, for an artificial smile is the saddest sight on earth. We all know people who carry a fixed, frozen, mirthless, almost professional, smile. Really, however, that is not a smile at all, it is just a permanent wave in the face.

Smile, even if it takes a little effort at first, and keep it up until it becomes spontaneous, as it will. In the graphic language of Hollywood, *register joy, and hold it!*

Rough Altars

T he secret of success in prayer is to be *simple, direct,* and *spontaneous.* Any kind of elaboration is sure to break the spiritual contact and result in failure. In the above text, the Israelites were told that they must not polish, or square, or otherwise elaborate their altars; they were to use just a rough and ready pile of stones.

Israel in the Bible stands for anyone who believes in God and in prayer, and so we see from this text that effective prayer is something direct and immediate.

As soon as you begin to elaborate, you are using the intellect, and with the intellect you cannot get spiritual contact. The intellect is an excellent thing within its own strictly limited sphere, but you cannot *pray* intellectually. Whenever your mental activity becomes involved, especially if you feel that you are being rather clever or literary, you may be enjoying yourself, but be certain that you are not praying.

If a tiger suddenly jumped in the window, you would not elaborate or plunge into abstract metaphysical speculations; you would pray very directly, and you would probably make your demonstration.

33

There is a very practical lesson in this example. The reason people usually get the most remarkable answers to prayer in times of great emergency is that it is at such times that they are *simple, direct,* and *spontaneous.*

Faith

Verily, I say unto you, If ye have faith, and doubt not, ye shall not only do this which is done to the fig tree, but also if ye shall say unto this mountain, be thou removed, and be thou cast into the sea; it shall be done.

—MATTHEW 21:21

An understanding faith is the life of prayer. It is a great mistake, however to struggle to produce a lively faith within yourself. That can only end in failure. The thing to do is to *act as though you had faith.* What we voluntarily do will always be the expression of our true belief. Act out the part that you wish to demonstrate, and you will be expressing true faith. "Act as though I were, and I will be," says the Bible in effect. This is the right use of the will, scientifically understood.

The statement of Jesus quoted above is perhaps the most tremendous spiritual pronouncement ever made. Probably no other teacher who ever lived would have dared to say it, but Jesus knew the law of faith and proved it himself many times. We shall move mountains when we are willing to believe that we can, and then not only will mountains be moved, but the whole planet will be redeemed and re-formed according to the Pattern in the Mount.

Know the Truth about your problems. Claim spiritual dominion. Avoid tenseness, strain, and over-anxiety. Expect your prayer to be answered, and *act* as though you expected it.

35

Building and Wrecking

To solve a problem, or to bring some good into your life, you have to make a new mental "set-up" concerning the matter in question. Paul tells us that we are *transformed by the renewing of our minds.* Indeed, a large part of what we call treatment is really the building up of a new mental attitude in this way. You have to break down the old mental concept and carefully build up a new one, just as an old building has to be torn down before a new one can go up on the same site.

Many people understand all this in principle, but they fail to demonstrate because they do not carry it out logically in practice. During the treatment, they carefully build up the new mental structure, but as soon as the treatment is over, instead of faithfully preserving that structure intact long enough for it to materialize in the outer, they promptly knock it down again by negative thinking. It is as though a bricklayer should devote the morning to building a wall and then spend the afternoon knocking down what he had built. Obviously, he could work hard in this fashion year after year without ever accomplishing anything.

If this seems to be happening to you, it is probably due to the same cause—building followed by wrecking. We are transformed by the *renewing* of our minds.

Flee to the Mountains

*When ye therefore shall see the abomination of desolation,
spoken of by Daniel the prophet, stand in the holy place,
(whoso readeth, let him understand:) Then let them which be
in Judea flee into the mountains: Let him which is on the
housetop not come down to take any thing out of his house:
Neither let him which is in the field return back to take his
clothes.*

—MATTHEW 24:15–18

T he moment you catch yourself thinking a negative thought, you should reject it instantly. Immediately switch your attention to the Presence of God. Do not stop to say "goodbye" to the error thought, but break the connection instantly and occupy your mind with good; you will be surprised how many difficulties will begin to melt away out of your life. Indeed, we may say that when error presents itself to consciousness, the first five seconds are Golden.

In the text quoted above, Jesus teaches this lesson in his own graphic way. The immediate application of these words was, of course, to the coming siege of Jerusalem, but the idea involved is eternal. The holy place is your consciousness, and the abomination of desolation is any negative thought, because a negative thought means belief in the absence of God at the point concerned. Those who are in Judea are those who believe that prayer does change things; to flee to the mountains means to pray, especially that quick switching of the thought to the Presence of God, which I have mentioned.

The dramatic detail with which the lesson is illustrated
makes it impossible that we should ever forget it when
once we have the spiritual key.

Personality, True and False

The term *personality* is one that has been greatly misunderstood in the metaphysical movement. It is often used as being synonymous with error, but no greater mistake can be made. Indeed, this misconception is probably the sole cause of a good many failures to demonstrate. When things go wrong, people often say, "that is a case of personality," when they really mean *false* personality.

Personality, rightly understood, is God's expression on this plane. Your individuality is your spiritual identity, but this has to be expressed on the physical plane, and that expression is seen as personality. When the expression is clear and logical, we get a brilliant and well-balanced personality, which means true success in life. Such a person is found to be unselfish, high-minded, and extremely efficient in his own field.

On the other hand, when the expression of the individuality or Christ-man is clouded, confused, and illogical, we see selfishness, confusion, and failure in the personality. Sometimes we also get either a very negative, drifting type of character, or perhaps an aggressive, overbearing, egotistical type.

Do not try to get rid of personality, but develop your personality on scientific and spiritual lines. *Human personality is not to be destroyed, but redeemed.*

One World—Not Two

Many students of metaphysics fall into the vital error of thinking that there are two worlds: a world of limitation and trouble "down here," and another world of perfection "somewhere up there." It is probable that they do not always visualize their mistake as clearly as this, but that they do labor under such a delusion is evident from the remarks they often make when off their guard.

Watch your own phraseology and notice whether you speak as though you thought there were two worlds; if you do, you must hasten to correct that view.

The truth is that there is one world—God's world—spiritual and perfect now, but that we see it in a limited and often distorted way owing to our false beliefs, and this distorted view of the real world is the so-called world of limitation. By practicing the Presence of God wherever distortion shows itself, you will rapidly redeem your own existence and help to liberate the whole race too.

"Great Sacred Cow—Do Not Touch!"

T he searchlight of Truth must be brought to play upon every phase of your life if you want complete, all round demonstration. No corner must be overlooked. You must be prepared to reconsider everything in your life, from top to bottom, in terms of your new understanding. Beliefs, habitual activities, home and business arrangements, family relationships, all must be revised from time to time. If present arrangements are of long standing, that is no reason for allowing them to continue; it is an excellent reason for revising and changing them for the better.

Most people have certain sections of their lives where, for various reasons (mostly unknown to themselves), they do not wish to make any change. These places are set aside and surrounded with an aura of spurious sanctity like the sacred cows of the East, which are considered too holy to be touched. But this kind of thing has to go. If you really mean business about regenerating your soul and body, there must positively be no sacred cows in your life. Nothing must be considered too sacred or too long established for revision, reconsideration, or, usually best of all, flinging out altogether.

The sacred cow is the most deadly form of the sin of idolatry. *Nothing is truly sacred but your own Indwelling Christ and the process of His awakening.* "Awake thou that sleepest and arise from the dead, and Christ shall give thee light."

It Cannot Be Your Duty

I f you are living the spiritual life, you are entitled to peace of mind and harmonious progress. Should these things seem to be lacking, have a mental stock-taking and ask Divine Wisdom to show you the reason for the lack.

It is your duty to set aside a reasonable time each day for prayer and spiritual reading, and to live the rest of your life in accordance with what your innermost self tells you is the Divine Will. That is to say, *as far as is possible for you at the moment.* If you are sincerely doing this, you can do no more, and you have no cause for anxiety or self-reproach because you are not accomplishing what is at present impossible for you.

It cannot be your duty to do anything that is beyond your reach or your strength at the moment.

It cannot be your duty to do anything that you do not have time to do.

It cannot be your duty to pay any sum of money that you do not possess.

It cannot be your duty to do anything that sacrifices your own integrity or your own spiritual development.

It cannot be your duty to do today what is really the task of tomorrow.

It cannot be right to perform a remote duty at the sacrifice of a nearer one.

It cannot be right to be hurried, or sad, or discouraged, or angry, or resentful, or antagonistic, under any circumstances.

"All Things Be Ready If
Our Minds Be So"

T his is one of the greatest statements of spiritual law ever made. Even in the pages of the Bible itself there is no clearer or more definite guidance in the art of living. Shakespeare here gives us a complete statement of metaphysical truth. Every student of this science should write it in letters of fire upon his heart. It is the door of freedom and the Jacob's ladder from earth to heaven.

There is nothing in the universe that you cannot do or be if you are mentally ready. People speak of golden opportunities, but what we call opportunity is really one's own mental readiness. Napoleon said, "Opportunities? I *make* opportunities." And while this would be merely a vainglorious boast for one who is not on the spiritual basis, yet when you do understand the Truth of Being, it is simply a statement of fact. The Romans could have had the telephone, the Greeks could have had the cinema, the Babylonians could have had the automobile—had they been mentally ready. The laws of nature were the same in those ages as in ours, the same materials were in the ground—but the minds of the Ancients were not ready for those things, and so they had to go without them.

We say in metaphysics that demand and supply are one, and it is equally true that supply and demand are one also. Supply the necessary mental condition, and the demand, the opportunity, or the occasion, will present itself automatically.

Whenever you are ready you will find that everything else is ready too.

Christopher Columbus

A merican Truth students should never forget that the primary object of the existence of the United States is to spread throughout the world the Truth of the Omnipresence and Availability of God.

It is no mere coincidence that the discoverer of America was named *Christopher Columbus*. We know that, rightly understood, "the name is the nature," and, as everybody knows, the name Christopher means belonging to the Christ, and the name Columbus means concerning a dove. Now, the Christ is the Spiritual Truth about anything, the knowing of which will heal any limitation, and the dove is, of course, the universal symbol of the Holy Spirit, which is the direct inspirational action of God in the individual soul.

So the name of America's discoverer is a complete crystallization of the Jesus Christ message. This wonderful hieroglyphic implies the Allness of God, the power of Scientific Prayer, and the fact of man's direct contact with the Divine Mind without the need for any outside mediator, whether it be a man or an institution.

This is why the United States has to be a democratic country, and why, among other things, it must always stand for the maximum of personal freedom for the individual.

Spotlights

We never fail because we are too good—only because we are not good enough.

To recognize failure intelligently is the first step toward building success.

Recognize success with thanksgiving and build more success on that.

You can have anything in life that you really want, but you must be prepared to take the responsibilities that go with it.

To solve any problem, get a little higher in consciousness.

Praying for inspiration is just as important as healing a condition.

When you resist a difficulty, you antagonize it, and it hits back.

Do not wrestle with the error—know it is not there.

Peace of mind first—and all things will follow on that.

God is ready the moment you are.

No Waiting

D on't wait about for God to act dramatically—because He won't. If you want anything to happen, you must bring about a change in your own mental outlook, whereupon your outer experience will automatically change to correspond. When people expect a dramatic miracle from the outside, they are really hoping to change conditions without changing themselves—to get something for nothing, in fact, and that would be a violation of Cosmic Law.

Don't wait for God to tell you what to do from the outside—He won't. People have said to me, "Well, I am ready. Whatever God wants me to do, I am ready. If He wants me to go to California, or to Europe, or to start any work for Him, I am ready." Such people, I have noticed, are apt to go on "being ready" indefinitely without anything ever happening. The fact is that they are waiting for a dramatic experience such as came to Moses on Sinai, and to Paul on the road to Damascus. Or probably they expect a Western Union boy to arrive with a telegram of instructions from heaven. None of these things will happen.

If you are really "ready to do God's work," you will have a clear idea of what you are going to do and how you propose to go about doing it, and probably you will know approximately where you are going to do it too. *This is being ready.* If you do not have any definite desire or plan, then you are not "ready"; so don't deceive yourself but get ready by treating for guidance. Treat for guidance, inspiration, wisdom, and right activity, until you have a clear, vivid, and whole-hearted enthusiasm for a definite plan. Then you will really be ready to do the Lord's work, and if you vitalize your plan with unceasing treatment, nothing can prevent your success.

Me Bothers I

Do not identify yourself with your present mentality any more than with your body. The real you is the "Christ within" or the "I am." When your body gives you pain or trouble, you handle it as best you can, knowing that it is something distinct from yourself; you should do the same with your mind. Say every morning: "I am not my body. I am not my thoughts. I am not my feelings. I am Divine Spirit, an individualization of God." To realize in this way that you are not one with your present mentality, but that it is only your instrument, makes it possible for you to change it for the better very rapidly.

When you find it difficult to manage yourself, think "I" intend to think rightly, but "me" does not want to; nevertheless "me" will have to do what "I" want—I am boss.

Of course "me" can be very troublesome, but as soon as you handle it objectively in this way it knows it is beaten and quickly surrenders. I want to get up but me wants to lie in bed. Or me claims indigestion, although I know I have dominion over my body. Or me is hurt and angry and wants to hit back, although I am determined to forgive. Or me says that business is hopeless, when I know that God is my supply. This is how the battle presents itself to consciousness, but as long as I insist that I am divine, God's own expression, I must and shall win.

Swing Doors to Hell

Both heaven and hell are states of consciousness, the net resultant of our beliefs and feelings at any time. Formerly, people thought that both heaven and hell were places where one went after death, and nowadays many people seem to think that neither heaven nor hell exists at all. The truth is that both hell and heaven do exist, but they are states of mind, and we experience them right here on this earth now.

When you have true peace of mind and an adequate understanding of life, you are already in heaven; when you are full of fear, anxiety, hatred, or physical pain, you are in hell. The conventional descriptions of both places are but an attempt to provide symbolic pictures of states of mind.

Whether you are to live in hell or in heaven depends solely upon the kind of thinking you indulge in all day long. And, fortunately, you can, by taking a little trouble, train yourself to make heavenlike thinking a constant habit.

The doors of hell are swing doors. There are no locks or fastenings upon them. They swing in or out at a push, and you can go inside any time you choose to do so, and, by the same token, you can also come out again any time you choose.

The way out of hell is to begin thinking thoughts of health, happiness, and success at this very moment, and to keep it up hour after hour and day after day in spite of all appearances. If only you will do this with determination, you will be through the swing doors and out of your difficulties before you know what has happened.

Leaves from the Fool's Handbook*

1. How to Be Unhappy
Sit down quietly where you are not likely to be disturbed. Relax the body—and begin to think about *yourself*. It does not matter very much what you actually think, as long as it is about yourself. Think about yourself, and every time your thought wanders to something higher, bring it back gently but relentlessly.

If possible think about the past. Think over all the mistakes you have ever made, going right back to childhood. Think of all the foolish things you have ever said or done. Think over all the opportunities you have missed and the time you have wasted. Especially think of all the occasions upon which you have been badly treated. Consider carefully the various injustices of which you have been the victim and think how much better off you might be in various ways today if other people had only behaved properly in times gone by. Remind yourself vividly of the unkind things that people have done to you and rehearse the incidents in detail, feeling as angry or hurt as you possibly can at each recollection. Even if a particular person has never actually offended you, realize that he might have done so if he had had the chance, and tell yourself that he has probably talked about you anyway.

*A fool in the Bible usually means a person who will not make use of the intelligence that God gives him. See Psalm 14:1; Proverbs 10:21; 18:2; 18:7; Ecclesiastes 7:6.

Think about your body and wonder if your age or your job or the climate isn't beginning to tell. See if you cannot discover a pain or an ache somewhere; you probably can if you search long enough.

Think about business or finances as gloomily as possible and even if they are going well now, insist that this is probably too good to last.

In any case, think about *yourself,* that is the main point, and if you will keep this up faithfully for fifteen or twenty minutes, there can be no doubt about the result. You will have attained your goal.

2.

How to Fail in Everything

Knock everything systematically. No matter what you hear of, depreciate it and predict the worst. This will build up an inferiority complex in yourself that will inevitably destroy any good thing in your life that you otherwise might allow to slip by.

Mind everyone else's business. This will ensure your neglecting your own.

Try to please everyone and take everyone's advice. This will leave your mind in complete chaos.

Try to live on bluff. You are certain to be found out before long, and then no one will respect you again.

Believe everything you hear. Someone said it, so, of course, it must be true.

When you get a good idea, run about and tell everyone. This gives them a chance to discourage you by throwing cold water on it, and it causes your own spiritual energy to leak away like a ground in an electric circuit.

Never perform today what you can possibly postpone until tomorrow.

Leave the important things to someone else instead of seeing to them personally.

Make a point of arriving the day after the fair.

Have no organized arrangements. Trust to luck for everything.

The day after the fire is the best time to insure.

Avoid notebooks and rely on memory.

Never be original. Find out what is usually done and copy that.

Realize that you have nothing more to learn. This will destroy all danger of success.

Give yourself airs and high-hat everybody. This will make you universally unpopular.

Sneer at those who are more successful than yourself. This will have a particularly damaging effect on your own life.

Tell yourself that it is now too late and that you really did not have the proper equipment, and it will be especially helpful to keep saying that people are against you.

Never learn from experience. Keep on doing the same darn fool things time after time.

Never wait to hear the other side of the story. Knowing both sides will only unsettle your mind.

Use your wit destructively. Be smart at the expense of absent people. This is sure to be carried to them and will make enemies for you.

Stand on your dignity. Never forget that you have a position to keep up, even if you have nothing to keep it up on. Never do any work that is not just to your liking. This policy should bring you safely into the bread line.

Try to get everything on the cheap. Beat down everyone. Study and practice to become the perfect "chiseler." This will build an invincible poverty complex.

Be a sanctimonious humbug, and when you bungle things, say it is "the Lord's will" or that the trouble is that you are too good for your surroundings.

Sit down and wait for something to turn up. This is the sovereign recipe for failure.

Finally, conduct your life in all respects as if there were no God.

| **3.** | How to Destroy Your Health |

Neglect your health completely. Take good care of your dog and your horse and your automobile, but your body is not important.

Fuss about your health all the time. Think of nothing else. Carry a clinical thermometer and take your temperature and your pulse every few hours. This sort of thing will destroy any constitution.

Get emotional and excited over every trifling occurrence, especially if it is no concern of yours.

Eat and drink indiscriminately anything that comes along. Your stomach is only a sink, anyway, and being made of cast iron, will stand anything.

Cut down your sleep. This is an excellent way to undermine the nervous system.

Never relax. That would give the body a chance to recuperate.

Avoid all exercise. Exercise promotes circulation and builds up health.

Breathe in shallow, irregular spasms. Deep, rhythmical breathing renews the whole organism.

Be as critical as you can of others, and if possible try to feel mean and resentful. This will be very helpful.

Read as much as you can about diseases and ailments in general. Your public library will carry many suitable books for this.

Discuss your own ailments at great length and, if you have had an operation, give dramatic little lectures about it at every opportunity.

Despise your body, or, better still, pretend you haven't got one at all. The Bible says that your body is the Temple of the Holy Spirit, and to go against the Bible is always a good short cut to trouble.

Treatment or Scientific Prayer

Treatment means knowing the Spiritual Truth about any person or situation.

If, like most people, you believe that appearances are realities and that they cannot be changed, then you cannot give a treatment. But if you believe that Jesus was right when he said, "Judge not according to appearances but judge *righteous* judgment," it is in your power to change anything for the better and to heal most things.

Begin every treatment (no matter how many you may give) by saying:

Treatment can overcome this difficulty.

I have nothing to deal with but my own thoughts.

Then get to work on these thoughts and change them—one by one if necessary—from error to Truth. Insist on the good and harmonious character of Being. Insist that God really is the only Presence and the only Power. Remind yourself constantly that your own concept is what you see, and that it is your business to change that. Make "me" toe the line and show him that "I" am the boss. Claim *power* as the child of God.

Be persistent. Do not take "no" for an answer, and it can only be a matter of time before you are victorious.

Casting the Burden

W e sometimes hear the expression used, "cast the burden," and it is useful to consider what this phrase really means. Used intelligently, it is one of the great keys to spiritual victory, but without intelligence it is just a meaningless platitude. To cast the burden means really to insist upon harmony and peace of mind, and to cease from worry and anxiety there and then. This leaves you free to go about your business in a serene frame of mind, following upon which, in due course, you find your problem solved.

As a student of metaphysics you know that evil is an unreal, temporary experience, and that fear is a bluffer. You know that health, happiness, and joy are eternal and are completely yours *now*. You know that because this fact is the Cosmic Law of God it cannot be changed. No matter what seems to have happened, harmony and perfection are the fact. And to hold on to this truth means that experiencing the demonstration will only be a matter of time.

If, when you are faced with trouble, whether it be old or new, you can affirm positively the Harmony of Being as expressed in the above paragraph, and then refuse to reopen the case, no matter how much fear may urge you to do so, *you have cast your burden upon the Lord*, and you will win.

58

My Steer

Y ou cannot claim too much for yourself provided you claim the same thing for all other human beings. In fact, it is your duty to claim all good things and to continue claiming them until they demonstrate in your outer experience. Claim health. Claim harmony and true success. Claim happiness. Claim power to help and bless others. Above all, claim power in prayer, the power to demonstrate in your own life.

You need not be afraid that this policy can cause you to be egotistical or selfish. On the contrary, it will make you a blessing to all with whom you come in contact. Of course, this law works both ways (it would not be a law if it did not), and therefore you must be very careful not to claim the negative things that you do *not* want.

On the western ranches the owner of a steer brands it with his name, "Bar A Ranch" or some such cipher. Then whenever he sees it he says *"my steer."* If it should wander into strange territory, it will always be returned to him. His brand is on it and it belongs to him. On the other hand, when an animal without his brand wanders into his corral, he says, "That is not my steer," and out it goes.

Many a foolish person puts his mental brand on a steer that he does not want in the least, and is surprised and disappointed when the animal stays obstinately at home. People say *my* rheumatism, *my* forgetfulness, *my* poverty, and so forth, branding the steers they do not want instead of disowning them and turning them out of the corral.

Keep your mental branding iron for the things that you want, and when you really want something, brand it deeply with your own name and it will be yours.

The Door That Opens In

T he door of the soul opens inward. That is often the reason we do not make our demonstration. We assume that it opens outward and we press and push against it as hard as we possibly can, seemingly oblivious of the fact that we are really but closing it all the more firmly against our good.

To work in this way is really to use will power, which is not treatment at all. It is simply trying to overcome by human effort and leaving God out.

Human nature is very prone to push blindly when frightened or frustrated. Indeed, this is precisely why the doors on all theaters and other public buildings are obliged by law to open outward—because it is the natural direction of panic. Prayer, however, is essentially the refusal to be rushed by panic or by the existing current of things. In prayer, you must draw back from the outer picture, cease to press against events, and realize the Presence of God. *The door of the soul opens inward.*

Why Does Not God . . . ?

Most of the difficulties that people experience concerning religion are traceable to two or three basic misunderstandings, and once these points are thoroughly cleared up it will be found that the majority of such problems solve themselves.

The most common mistake is to think of God as being just a big man—very big, very wise, very good, but still a big man—managing the world from the outside. Many of us think we have gotten beyond this, but it turns out that in our hearts we really have not. So we say: Why did God allow the World War to happen? Why do we have strikes, and floods, and riots? What about the terrible civil war in Spain? Why did God allow Aunt Jane or Cousin George to suffer so tragically? Of course, this really means, "If I were God, I would have put these things right," and this in itself gives us a clue.

God is Infinite Mind, the great Over-soul, and man is the individualization of the Great Mind, having intelligence and free will, and therefore the power to make his own conditions. When he uses his mental powers wrongly, he produces fear, hatred, greed, and all kinds of error, and these in turn demonstrate themselves as war, sickness, poverty, and so forth.

The only way to abolish such evil things is to change the race mind by getting rid of the negative thoughts that cause them, and this can be done by Scientific Prayer. Then these thoughts, having disappeared from people's minds, can no longer demonstrate themselves in the outer. In other words, war, crime, and disease will vanish, and those who are praying every day for the peace of the world are now actually bringing this about.

You will see that this is the only way it can be done, and that if an outside God could pull the strings in the way thoughtless people wish, we should be only puppets or marionettes. Then your life would not be the Great Adventure that it is, and where would be the fun of living?

The Mills of God

A nother basic error that misleads many people is this—they think of God and man in terms only of the moment, or, at most, of a few years. They want to see everything squared up and settled within a year or two and because this does not happen, they decide that there is no justice in the universe, no law and order, and they wonder why God does not step in and do something about it.

Now, you are going to live forever—somewhere. You are going to live, not for a century or a thousand centuries, but forever. And so you will see that a year or two, or twenty or thirty years, is a very short time in which to look for permanent results. *The mills of God grind slowly but they grind exceeding small.* The gardener does not say that there is no law in nature because his crop does not come up a week after he sows it. We do not say that the railroad has broken down because the train is not in Chicago half an hour after it leaves New York, but we are often tempted to think that there is no law of justice and righteousness because we do not see the results of people's good or evil deeds very soon after they happen.

Whatsoever a man soweth, says the Bible, that shall he also reap. This reaping takes time. If it seems to you that in your own life you have not received your desserts, the answer is that the end is not yet. If it seems that someone else known to you is not getting either the rewards or the punishments that you consider him entitled to, the answer is—the end is not yet. God is never mocked, and sooner or later every prayer is answered. Every good thought, or word, or deed produces its fruit of happiness and spiritual advancement, and, of course, every negative thing for which we are responsible will have to be met and overcome also. Nature always takes her time, and to understand her you must take the long view too.

Pike's Peak or Bust!

There is no condition that cannot be overcome with sufficient spiritual power. There is no problem that can present itself to the mind of man that cannot be solved with enough spiritual understanding. The very fact that man can become conscious of a problem at all is a proof that he can find a solution. We are here on the earth to solve these very problems, because in solving them we develop our own spiritual faculties. Every difficulty that comes into your life, every problem that presents itself to you, means that here is a point at which you are to learn something.

Do not be an idolater and worship difficulties, as many people do. When you say that some trouble is insurmountable, or that a problem is insoluble, you are an idolater and you are denying your own divine selfhood. Let nothing intimidate you. As the expression of God you are more than equal to anything that may arise, if only you have *courage* and *faith*.

Most heathen countries have a "holy mountain." This really means that coming upon a particularly high and inaccessible locality, the people lost their courage, allowed themselves to be overawed, and, instead of tackling and conquering the difficulty, they fell on their knees in abject terror and rubbed their foreheads on the ground, saying, "Oh, holy mountain, do not hurt us."

In America we have no holy mountains of this kind. It is not our custom to grovel before difficulties but to conquer them. Coming upon a fifteen thousand foot mountain, the western pioneers did no groveling. Instead, they said, *"Pike's Peak or bust,"* and they got to the top of the mountain and conquered it, instead of letting the mountain conquer them. To do this is to glorify God, instead of lapsing into idolatry.

Do not have any holy mountains in your life. Do not allow any difficulty, no matter what it is, to scare you. Say *"Pike's Peak or bust"* and go at it and conquer it.

The real Holy Mountain, as the Bible knows it, is the uplifted consciousness that has dominion over all things, never a mountain in the outer world.

Don't Try—Let

People often say, "I try to do this," or, "I try to do that, but I fail," or, "I tried so hard but nothing came of it," and they become discouraged and dispirited. They wonder why things will not come right. And yet the explanation is contained within the words themselves.

You should never "try"; you should "let"—let God. When you "try" to do things, you are working from the outside. When you let God do them through you, you are working from the inside and success must come.

If you will re-read the creation chapter in the Bible (the first of Genesis) you will notice that God creates by "letting." God said, "Let there be light." God said, "let," at every act of creation, and it was done.

Now God creates by means of you if you will let him, but *you must let*. Remember that in all mental working *effort defeats itself*. The scientific way of working is to "let" God manifest through you the wonderful ideas that He gives to you from time to time.

Open your dictionary (in imagination) and scratch out the word "try" and write the word "let" against it in the margin.

Someone said, "Let go and let God," and this is a wonderful recipe for overcoming fear or getting out of a tight place. In any case, the rule for creation is always to *let*.

It's More Fun to Be Intelligent

I t is your duty to God to run your life on intelligent lines. God gives us all as much intelligence as we can possibly need, but, unfortunately, in most cases we use very little of it. We apply our intelligence only here and there in our lives instead of applying it at every point.

Ask yourself today if you are really conducting your life intelligently. Are you eating and drinking intelligently? Do you select your reading intelligently? Do you spend your money intelligently? Do you use the power of the Word intelligently by speaking only the positive and constructive things you wish to demonstrate? Do you think intelligently? Do you consider intelligently the things that you hear, or do you just accept them uncritically? Above all, do you bring intelligence to bear on the religion that you profess and judge it by that standard alone?

Do you really exercise intelligence in carrying out your daily work, whatever it may be? Do you seek to approach each new problem as it arises, with intelligence instead of mere emotion?

Have you intelligent plans for the future? Do you know what you would really like to do or to be, and if not, wouldn't it be only intelligent to go to work and find out, and then draw up an intelligent plan for gaining your desire?

What the world most needs today is more intelligence. There is plenty of good feeling and good will, but because people will not use enough intelligence, mankind everywhere is in difficulties. The real solution for world problems is for the mass of the people in every country to apply intelligence—setting aside prejudice and blind tradition—to political and economic problems, and when this is done a solution will surely be found. Meanwhile, each one of us can do this independently in his own life.

Your intelligence is the light of God in your soul. Do not muddle. Do not drift. Use your intelligence. *It is more fun to be intelligent.*

Come Off That Burning Deck!

Most people still remember the old poem about the Boy on the Burning Deck. That poem has a very important lesson for us all, though not quite the one the author intended.

The boy, you remember, stood still doing nothing, although the ship was on fire, and so the fire went on spreading until the ship finally blew up, killing all hands. Of course, no other result could be expected with such incompetent people on board, and it is no wonder that the whole battle was lost, if this incident represented the general spirit of the fleet.

An American or British boy would not have stood there wailing, but would have organized a bucket chain and put the fire out, or else taken whatever steps seemed best under the circumstances, evacuating the ship if necessary. And if any foolish sentimentalist had interfered, such person would have been put under control for his own and the public good.

Unfortunately, we come across a good many of these spurious Burning Deck Heroes in private life. Instead of attacking and overcoming their difficulties, they stand by looking at them helplessly. In reality they lack the courage and the intelligence to face up to the problem as it should be faced, but they comfort themselves by pretending that they are just being noble and self-sacrificing—adding hypocrisy to weakness and making the complete failure inevitable.

If you ever catch yourself at anything like this—if you find yourself posing as a martyr—you must have no mercy with such fatal weakness. Say to yourself: "Come off that burning deck, put the fire out, save the ship, and win the battle." And then it will be time to stand still and look heroic.

Don't Force Things

Never force things. Never bring heavy pressure to bear in a given direction. Never make up your mind that a certain thing *must* be done, or that it must be done *now.* All this sort of thing is dangerous, and is likely to land you in trouble instead of improving matters. It is really using will power, and is unscientific and unspiritual. It is looking to the without, whereas spiritual demonstration looks to the within. It is what engineers call a centripetal action, and spiritual demonstration is always centrifugal.

What you really want is harmony and true expression at every point in your life. The actual way in which this comes does not matter so long as you get the thing itself. When you encounter a firm resistance anywhere, it usually means that you are on the wrong road and had better retreat and try another. Mental or material pushing will only get you farther down the wrong road, and it gives you a longer distance to retrace.

Claim that God works in you, and that when He works He always succeeds, that He knows the best way and is inspiring you to take it, that He meets no resistance for He works with joy, and that you and your life are part of that.

Spotlights

He can who thinks he can.

Face the facts candidly—and then you can alter them.

Grumbling is a certain sign of weakness. Don't grumble—change the condition.

The two keys of success are originality and hard work. God will give you the first, through prayer, and the second is up to you.

Unless you have confidence in yourself, you are licked before you start.

Criticism of others is the hallmark of failure.

Never resent jealousy; it is the height of flattery. No one is ever jealous of a fool.

The One Thing That Matters

T he most important of all things to possess is Peace of Mind. There is absolutely nothing else in the world that is equal in value to that. Nothing else that life can offer is so important, and yet it seems to be about the last thing that many people work for. They strive both spiritually and materially for everything else under the sun, whereas, if they had everything else, and still lacked Peace of Mind, they would be miserable. If anyone should come to you with a billion dollars in one hand and Peace of Mind in the other, if you took the billion dollars, you would be the most foolish person on earth.

Peace of Mind includes all other good things. If you have this, it does not matter where you are or what surrounding conditions may be—all will be well. Even if the outer picture were an unpleasant one in itself, it would cause you no grief if you had Peace of Mind, and very soon that picture would inevitably change into something better.

Peace of Mind is positively the greatest of all God's gifts. Pray for this and the rest will take care of itself. "Peace I leave with you; my peace I give unto you," said Jesus, implying that this was the highest good he had to give us. And truly, *Peace of Mind is the one thing that matters.*

Produced Without Rehearsal

S omeone said that living your life is like playing a violin solo in public and learning to play the instrument as you go along. This is a true saying. It describes the experience very well, but no one should worry about that. We are in this world for exactly that purpose—to learn.

While you are learning you do not expect to produce a perfect work. When you can produce a perfect work you are a master and no longer a student. On this plane we are all students, and what matters is that each year we shall find the quality of our workmanship definitely better, proving that we are a step nearer to mastership.

People are sometimes depressed because their lives do not present a simple, logical, harmonious unfoldment— because their histories seem to be full of inconsistencies, repetitions, dead ends, and yawning gaps. This, however, is only to be expected during the learning period. At the beginning of the school year a child's exercise book is full of mistakes—at the end of the year there are hardly any mistakes, which means that he has finished with that grade and is ready to go up higher. If the early weeks showed an excellent copy-book, it would simply mean that the student was in the wrong grade.

It is only on the stage (and then only in a good play) that the action unfolds logically, evenly, tidily, compactly, to its conclusion. But, then, the actors in a play have no free will, for it has all been rehearsed many times. *Your life has not been rehearsed.* It is an adventure, and a discovery, and a training, and it is only the Final Goal, or *last state,* and not your present state that matters.

76

Bluebeard Draws the Line

We make spiritual progress by putting God into every corner of our lives. Most people on the spiritual path are willing to give God 95 percent of their lives, but there is often one little corner that they keep back. *There is something or other they do not want to change.* There is one corner where they do not wish the Divine Light to shine.

As often as not they are not fully conscious of this, because the Old Adam is so subtle that he persistently diverts their attention from the weak point. They refuse to contemplate the fact, they make some feeble excuse to themselves—or they postpone.

Bluebeard, you remember, kept open house, with the exception of one little room—*but there he drew the line.* His current wife, or any of the neighbors could go all over the premises and welcome, until they came to that one little room, the Bluebeard chamber, but that was forbidden. Yet that one little locked-up room contained the tragedy of the house.

See to it that you have no Bluebeard chamber in your soul where the Divine Light is never allowed to penetrate. The contents of the Bluebeard room need not be anything that we usually call horrible. It may just be selfishness, laziness, spiritual pride, or any of the more "respectable" but very deadly sins. It may be an old grudge or it may be prideful remorse.

Open every door in the house of your soul to God. Have no place where the light of His presence does not shine.

God Says Now

God's time for your demonstration is *now*. The time God wants you to be healed is *now*. The time God wants you to be prosperous is *now*. The time God wants you to have your right home is *now*. The time God wants you to be in your True Place is *now*. The Bible says that the Day of Salvation is *now*.

God is ready the moment you are. There is nothing to wait for except the changing of your own consciousness. People often make the mistake of saying, "I know my demonstration will come at the right time." But the only time to be harmonious and satisfied is now. Never postpone your good or you can go on doing so indefinitely through all eternity. The time to be happy is now and the place is here. Did not Jesus say, "The Kingdom of Heaven is at hand"? By this he meant close by.

Do not keep yourself out of the Kingdom of Heaven by making excuses or inventing postponements, but go to work and change your consciousness now, for it can all happen in a moment.

The Mixing Bowl

W hen you make a cake, you know that whatever you put into the mixing bowl will appear in the cake itself and, on the other hand, that unless a particular substance does go into the mixing bowl, it cannot appear in the finished article.

Everyone realizes this clearly in connection with a material object like a cake, but people often fail to see that the same process applies equally in the realm of mind. Such, however, is the case. The thoughts and beliefs that fill our minds ultimately appear in the cake of experience, and to realize this is to save oneself a lot of trouble. No one puts kerosene in the mixing bowl because no one wants it in the cake, for everyone knows that if it does enter the bowl, in the cake it will be.

Keep mental kerosene and other ill-tasting things out of your mental mixing bowl and then your cake will be worth eating.

You Are Always Treating

Y ou are continually "treating" your conditions with the thoughts that you hold
concerning them. What you really think
about anything is your "treatment" of that thing. Many
people have the idea that they are only "treating" when
they call it "treating," but no matter what you call it, *your
thought concerning any subject is a treatment.*

This is the reason visible conditions are always the expression of invisible thought. This is the explanation of
the great truth that your own concept is what you see.

Every day you treat your body, you treat your business,
you treat your family, and you treat the city and the state
and the nation and the world, by the kind of thoughts
you think concerning them.

If you will begin systematically to treat every side of
your life with a series of positive, correct thoughts, and
keep to this practice for even a few weeks, you will be
amazed to find how much everything will change for
the better.

Take God for Your Partner

Why not organize the business of living in a big way? Why creep along, as some people do, from one tiny stepping-stone to another, instead of striding out boldly? Why be content with poor health, uninteresting work, or restricted conditions, when many other people have already risen above these things?

There is a way out of limitation that never fails. It is simple. It calls for no formalities. It requires no money. It is obvious enough when you realize it, but it is strange how many people nevertheless overlook it. It is this, *take God for your partner.*

If you will really make God your business partner in every department of your life, you will be amazed at the quick and striking results that you will obtain. I have said that this partnership will cost no money, but I did not say it would not cost anything. As a matter of fact it will cost you a great deal, because the price will be your whole life—but it will be worth it. Of course, if you want God to be your partner, He will have to be the Senior Partner, and you will have to include Him in every corner and every phase of your life. If you are prepared to do this, the result will not be in doubt.

Most people would be thrilled to be able to go into partnership with some great industrial or financial magnate; they would feel that their future was assured. But here is a partnership with Infinite Wisdom and Infinite Power awaiting you. Take God for your partner.

The Dictaphone

Your destiny depends entirely upon your own *mental conduct*. It is the thoughts that you allow yourself to dwell upon all day long that make your mentality what it is, and your circumstances are made by your mentality.

You may think that you know this already, but if you do not act upon it, it is certain that you do not really know it. As a matter of fact, most people would be amazed to discover how much negative thinking they do indulge in, in the course of a day. Thought is so swift, and habit is so strong that, unless you are very careful, you will constantly transgress. Even your conversation may be much more negative than you suspect.

If such an experiment as the following were possible, the result would probably fill you with amazement.

Suppose that, quite without your knowledge, an invisible and weightless dictaphone were strapped on your shoulders the first thing tomorrow morning, and that you carried it about with you all day until the last thing tomorrow night, and that the disk therein recorded every word you said. Then suppose that this dictaphone record were played over to you so that every single word you had uttered for a whole day was repeated to you in cold blood. Well, if you are an average human being you would probably be a little embarrassed. Yet it really does happen that everything we say, and think, and do, is recorded—in the subconscious mind—and our daily experience is simply that record being played over to us by the Law of Being.

Never forget that the circumstances of your life tomorrow are molded by your mental conduct of today.

A Spiritual Treatment

A Spiritual Treatment is a change of mind. When the mind changes, the outer expression must change to correspond; indeed Paul says, "We are transformed by the renewing of our minds."

When a problem confronts us, then, the only thing necessary is to change our minds concerning the matter in question, and this we do by reminding ourselves of the Spiritual Truth about it, and continuing to do so until we get some degree of realization.

Often it is not possible to accomplish this at one attempt, and so we repeat it as often as may be necessary, until at last the goal is reached.

A Spiritual Treatment is a definite operation. Begin it; finish it; and then leave it alone until the next time— usually the next day. Do not nibble at the subject in between treatments, but try to forget it.

Remember that to God no problem is difficult, and that to Him conditions do not matter.

Let That Dog Alone!

"**M**ind your own business" is a good rule. It would probably be safe to say that more than half of the evil in the world is due to well meaning busybodies who just cannot refrain from interfering. Needless to say, such people never have harmony or success in their own lives, for it is an invariable rule that he who minds his neighbor's business, neglects his own.

All this is true, and we cannot recollect it too often, but in the deeper sense it is equally true that what a man minds—what he gives his attention to—always does become his business, and sometimes his destruction. When you interfere *mentally* in any condition, you involve your life in it to the extent of that interference. When you take sides *mentally*, or become emotional concerning the matter, and still more when you talk about it, and still more again when you do anything about it, you are making yourself a party to it and will have to take the consequences.

In other words, you cannot involve your thought in any subject without bringing the natural consequences upon yourself. You can call this involving yourself in the karma of that situation, if you like, but whatever you choose to call it, the fact will remain. To interfere *mentally* in any situation involves you in the consequences just as much as would a physical interference. Of course, where it is your duty to concern yourself in any matter, you must do so constructively and spiritually—and then the consequences to you can only be good.

84

The Bible says, "he that passeth by, and meddleth with strife belonging not to him, is like one that taketh a dog by the ears" (Proverbs 26:17). If, when those around you are talking negatively about something or someone, you chip in with your contribution to the witches' brew, you are taking a strange dog by the ears—so look out! If you get emotionally entangled in what is not your affair, through indignation, self-righteousness, hatred, or otherwise, you have seized the dog again, and you will have to pay for it. If you rush about interviewing, telephoning, busying yourself in the same spirit, you have tackled the dog once more—and he will bite. And even to *think* negatively concerning such matters in the secret chamber of your own heart, will bring you proportionate and natural punishment.

It is always right to think *rightly* about any person or situation, and if you do this many opportunities will come to you to help people practically too, without any breach of the law we have been considering, and without coming near the dangerous dog.

Only Your Own Thoughts

N o matter what problem you may have to face today, there is a solution, because *you have nothing to deal with but your own thoughts*. As you know, you have the power to select and control your thoughts, difficult though it may be at times to do so. As long as you think that your destiny is in the hands of other people, the situation is hopeless. People say: "It is useless for me to struggle because of such and such a reason. If only I had a profession. If only I had married someone else. If only I had not bought this business. If only I had gone abroad when I had the chance"—and so on.

But this is a vital mistake, because *you have nothing to deal with but your own thoughts.*

Remind yourself of this fact constantly. Repeat it to yourself a hundred times a day until you really do begin to grasp all that it means to you. Write it down where you will see it often. Have it on your desk, or wherever you work. Hang it in your bedroom where you will easily see it. Write it in your pocketbook. *Write it on your soul,* by constantly dwelling upon it. It will transform your life. It will lead you out of the land of Egypt and out of the House of Bondage. It will bring you to God.

No Office Hours

God has no office hours. There is never a time when God is unavailable. Day or night, summer or winter, God is always present—always ready to heal, to comfort, to inspire. It is not possible that you could turn to God in prayer without receiving help. It is not possible that you could ever find yourself anywhere where God was not fully present, fully active, able and willing to set you free from any difficulty.

The one thing required of you is that you shall turn to Him *whole-heartedly,* and that you shall expect Him to act. If you are not whole-hearted—if you pray with the feeling that if it does no good, at least it can do no harm—you can hardly expect results.

If you turn to God in prayer, without tension, without vehemence, but quietly, steadily, and persistently, results will come. The greater the emergency, the easier will it be to demonstrate, but you must be *whole-hearted,* for the double-minded man is unstable in all his ways.

The most powerful of all prayers is simply *"Be still, and know that I am God."*

The Single Eye

T rue simplicity is the master-key of spiritual understanding. This simplicity will be found to inhere in material conditions, but of course its fundamental root lies in one's mental outlook. Simplicity of thought will naturally be reflected in a general simplicity in the way of living and working. The heart that is fixed on many different things is never at peace, and it is to the heart at peace that the realization of God comes.

Mental simplicity consists in seeing the One Presence everywhere—in all things. This is the *Single Eye* of which Jesus spoke, and if we will but cultivate the Single Eye, all the less important things will automatically fall into place.

It is because we are all too involved in external and unimportant details that we so often overlook the Great Opportunity. Man will undergo incredible hardships in his search for the Holy Grail—but when God puts the Chalice to his lips he too often pushes it roughly away.

N o. 1. Mr. Atlas

It is proverbial that the troubles that worry us most are the ones we never have to meet. Countless people have been killed by misfortunes that never happened to them. This looks absurd on paper but it is tragically true in life. Of all the types of foolish people, Mr. Atlas probably takes the palm. Not satisfied with his own many troubles (and Mr. Atlas is certain to have a great many of his very own), he has to go about worrying over everybody else's problems too. The Greeks pictured him carrying the whole world on his own shoulders, bowed down under the intolerable weight, and this is a splendid symbol of what many people are doing today.

Mind your own business, Mr. Atlas. Hoe your own row, scrub your own doorstep, and that will give you quite enough to do—if you do it properly. Do not try to carry the burdens of the whole world. Such a policy will destroy you and will not help the world.

Leave something to God. After all, it is He who is responsible for the world, and not you. Has it ever occurred to you that if *you* had never been born, the world would have had to get along somehow, and that God would probably take care of everything quite well?

To worry over conditions that you cannot change is gratuitous folly. To get and to keep your own peace of mind, to do your own duties well, and to see the Presence of God in all men and things, is the surest way both to help the world and to make your own life divinely successful too.

Drop that globe, Mr. Atlas, and straighten up, and look at the sky.

P.S.—Does Mr. Atlas remind you at all of someone whose name you often sign?

N o. 2. Mrs. Fix-It
She is probably the most energetic member in the club and is well in the running for the presidency. Everyone knows her, and few indeed have managed to escape her attentions. She is indefatigable, inescapable, unsnubbable. Nothing discourages her; to mere hints she is impervious—she means so well. She doesn't interfere in cold blood, it is simply an instinct with her—*she must try to fix it*. She has been interfering from the moment of her birth, trying to put everything right, and, needless to say, usually making things worse, doing more harm than good in the long run.

She has a passion for putting the other fellow's house in order. In a very literal sense, I have known her, when a guest in a house, to actually proceed to re-arrange the furniture and the pictures, telling her hostess where she was wrong.

Of course, she manages her entire family. Her brothers and her sisters and her cousins and her aunts have to toe the line—*her line*. She prescribes their diet, tells them when they can afford a car and which model to buy, or puts her foot down and says that for the present they ought to walk. The education of their children is a constant preoccupation with her, and she often tries to censor their friendships too. God help her parents, for, as a rule, no human power can save them. And her colleagues, if she is in business, and her associates elsewhere, dread her approach, and flee if there is yet time.

Mrs. Fix-it has her good points, of course. She is apt to be as generous with her money as with her advice. She is nearly always disinterested, wanting nothing for herself, sincerely desirous only of helping others. Her basic error is love gone wrong, as love is so apt to, when not balanced by intelligence. Give Mrs. Fix-it the right thought, but for heaven's sake keep at a safe distance from her.

P.S.—Does Mrs. Fix-it remind you at all of someone whose name you often sign?

N o. 3. Sweet Alice (Ben Bolt)
She is, of course, no longer an actual member, but there is a beautiful plaque to her memory in the lobby of the club. It is felt that her untimely demise robbed the club of one of its most promising recruits. You remember her peculiarity, of course. *She was afraid of everyone.*

"She wept with delight when you gave her a smile,
And trembled with fear at your frown."

Nothing mattered to her except other people's opinion. Not what she was, but what other people thought about her, was the important thing.

Modern medical science would have called this a case of acute neurasthenia, and prescribed special diet, open air exercise, and so forth, but our grandparents were merely sentimental about it. After this we are not in the least surprised to hear that

"She lies under a stone."

Nothing else could be expected. Nor does it help a bit that the stone is

"In an old church-yard in the valley,"

though this was evidently thought to be important.

The fact that a beautiful air is attached to these foolish verses only shows how a false sentiment will try to conceal itself behind something good.

Do not be a slave to other people's opinion. Do what you know is right and care for no man's censure. *Serve God and fear no one.* It does not matter in the least whether you please other people; it matters that you are loyal to God and to your own soul. As a matter of fact, those who are always trying to please everyone, seldom succeed in pleasing anyone. They tear their emotional natures to pieces instead of building serenity and poise.

With God on your side you can fearlessly look the world in the face.

P.S.—Does Alice remind you at all of someone whose name you often sign?

N o. 4. See-Saw Simpson

In a popular novel of the last generation, there was a boy whom his comrades nicknamed See-Saw Simpson, because he was constantly changing his mind. He is now a middle-aged man and has been a prominent member of the club for many years; in fact, he is second vice-president.

Brother Simpson never knows his own mind for twenty-four hours at a time. He is usually of the opinion of the last person who has talked to him, but not infrequently he switches again as soon as he is alone once more. His drifting mentality simply cannot crystallize in any direction. In the words of the Bible, he is cursed with the curse of Reuben—*unstable as water, thou shalt not excel.* He is sincere, good-natured, and well meaning, but his character is so weak that he cannot take a definite attitude on any point and hold to it. He has no definite principles. He does not know where he stands on any subject, nor does anyone else.

The natural consequence of all this, of course, is that in business he has been a drifting failure, and that in all social relationships he is sure to be the one who is overlooked. No one trusts Brother Simpson because no one ever knows what he will do next. It is impossible to make satisfactory arrangements with him about anything, because the next time you see him he will have changed his mind and let you down. And very likely he will soon afterward change it back again.

Make up your mind. Do one thing or the other, but in Heaven's name do not see-saw about indefinitely. If you take a decisive step, you may be right or you may be wrong, but if you see-saw about, you are certain to be wrong.

If indecisiveness is your failing, practice making snap decisions in the following way: When the occasion arises say, *the Christ is guiding me,* and then do one thing or the other *quickly.* Then stick to your choice, in spite of any doubts you may have to the contrary. If you really believe what you have said, that the Christ is guiding you, your decision must be the right one. Keep this practice up for some weeks and, while you will make mistakes in the beginning, you will rapidly find yourself making quick and almost effortless decisions that turn out to be correct, and this will become a habit.

P.S.—Does See-Saw Simpson remind you at all of someone whose name you often sign?

N o. 5. Wilbur Weakfish

He is easily the most popular member of the club. Everyone likes him. He is so kind. Indeed, his kindness is a byword among his friends, and most of them say he is the nicest man they ever met, a real good sport with a heart as big as his body.

He is indeed very kind to *almost* everyone—and in that "almost" lies the tragedy, for it gives the other side of the story.

Wilbur Weakfish is always popular with strangers because he cannot say *no* to them. It is only those who are nearest to him who ever hear that word. He is so full of philanthropy that there is no room in him for the word *duty*. He gives money to strangers because he cannot say *no,* although his wife needs a winter coat. He presents the club with a new set of bookcases for the library, for which he receives an illuminated address of thanks from the president, handed to him at a full meeting—but the landlord does not get his rent for a couple of months and the family is humiliated and threatened with dispossession.

He likes to see his name high up on every subscription list, but a large sum of money that he borrowed from his brother nearly ten years ago has never been repaid, and when his eldest boy was ready to enter college there was no money for him, and he had to find a job instead.

Why does he do it? People say it is because he is kindhearted. Nothing of the sort. It is because he is selfish and weak. He loves to be thanked effusively, to play Lord Bountiful, and one does not get this for doing one's duty. He cannot say *no* because he does not want to. He prefers to enjoy himself at anyone's expense.

P.S.—Does Wilbur Weakfish remind you at all of someone whose name you often sign?

N o. 6. Calamity Jane

She is the most regular attendant at club meetings, but even there she cannot be said to be popular, and everywhere else she is disliked. She is almost a hereditary member because her uncle, Dismal Daniel, was one of the founders of the club, although he said at the time that he did not think it could succeed. He underestimated the potential membership.

Calamity Jane is a chronic pessimist. She sees the dark side of everything immediately, and nothing else. She always anticipates the worst. When anything new is started, she says it cannot succeed, or that it is now too late. And when things are obviously going well, she shakes her head mournfully and says they are too good to last. Her role in life seems to be to discourage, as far as she can, everyone she comes across, and she is usually fairly successful in this. She is a born wet blanket; joy cannot live in her presence. No matter how enthusiastic people may be, Jane's arrival lowers the temperature toward zero.

According to Jane the country is shot to pieces and cannot recover. The state in which she lives has no future because the climate is bad and the soil is exhausted, and her city, she says, is doomed, because it is badly situated anyway, and those who govern it are a bunch of crooks.

Of course her own life is beset with constant difficulties. Her health is poor. She grumbles ceaselessly about her whole digestive tract, which is naturally in a bad way, and causes her daily torment, and she says there is no hope for it because it runs in the family and that her uncle Daniel had just the same trouble. Her financial and business affairs are so involved that they make her life a constant misery. She never knows where next month's rent is coming from, and sometimes this applies to last month's rent as well. Of course she can no more have prosperity than she can have health, with the mental model she has built for herself. But she seems incapable of realizing this, and goes on destroying her own health, happiness, and prosperity day after day. She is the only enemy that she has in the world.

P.S.—Does Calamity Jane remind you at all of someone whose name you often sign?

T he second best prayer ever written is the Scotsman's prayer—"Lord, give us a good conceit of ourselves." You cannot have too much respect for yourself. You cannot have too much confidence in yourself. You cannot claim too much for yourself. But remember that you must realize these things as being the expression of God in you and not independent qualities of your own. You must also accept them as being true for every other human being.

Nothing but failure can come of self-depreciation. Thinking of yourself as "a worm and the son of a worm" is the quickest way to demonstrate a wormy existence. Crawling about mentally can only be the prelude to crawling about spiritually, morally, and even physically. Affirm your Divine Selfhood, look the world in the face, and fear nothing.

Of course it is true that stupid people can get the malady called "swelled head"—and this always ends in a fall—but the realization of one's *Divine* Selfhood never gives swelled head. It gives wisdom, balance, poise, and steady progress.

Claim your Divine, Glorious Selfhood. Think it, talk it, live it, and it will demonstrate itself in your life. Come out of the mental dog house and move into the palace not made with hands—the palace of mental poise, divine wisdom, and true satisfying success.

Don't Talk About It

Never tell people about the fine thing you are going to do, but wait until you have done it and then show them the completed article. Never point to an empty lot and say: "I am going to build a tower there" but wait until the edifice is complete, and then if you like, say: "Look at the tower I have built." But when the tower is there it will not really be necessary to say anything at all, because it will speak for itself.

Talking about your plans before they have actually materialized, is the surest way to destroy them. It is a universal law of nature that the unborn child is protected from all contact with the world; in fact this is the real function of motherhood. Now the inspiration that comes to you is your child; you are its mother; and nature intends that you should protect and nourish that idea in secrecy and shelter, up to the moment when it is ready to emerge upon the material plane. To chatter or boast about it is to expose it to the world and kill it.

This applies to any new enterprise that you may be contemplating, as well as to a new idea. An important business deal, for instance, a large sale, the buying of a house, the forming of a partnership should be protected in the same way. Don't discuss these things at the lunch table or anywhere else.

Keep your business to yourself. Of course it is quite permissible to consult experts, and to reveal your plan where it is absolutely necessary to do so. This is nourishing the idea, not exposing it. It is chatter, gossip, and boasting that are to be avoided. *In quietness and confidence shall be your strength.*

What Do You Want?

A strong wish for something is the Voice of God in your heart urging you to take the next step forward. That is the way in which the Great Mind is communicating with you at the moment. A strong wish is a sacred thing to be received with the greatest respect and handled with the highest wisdom.

Many people have the false idea that their own wishes are sure to be mistaken and contrary to the Will of God. On this ground they repress all such wishes automatically and wait about for God to do something. This policy means complete stagnation and disappointment.

A strong wish is the Voice of God. It is true that you may be misinterpreting it in general, or misunderstanding it in detail, but that can be corrected by praying for wisdom. It is probable that 90 percent of your wishes are fundamentally right, and for any right wish, there is a fulfillment, because demand and supply are one.

Leave the details to God, but pray systematically for the general idea. For instance, if a townsman has a strong and continued wish to live in the country, he should pray for this to happen, but he should not concentrate on a particular house or farm. If a man has a strong and continued wish to start a business of his own, this is probably the Voice of God, and that Voice should be answered with systematic prayer—but he should not concentrate on a particular shop or even a particular locality.

True wishes have wings and will bear you to your heart's desire.

What Then?

othing is really worth worrying about. Nothing is really worth getting angry or hurt or bitter about. Positively nothing is worth losing your peace of mind over.

These important truths follow logically upon the following fact:

You are going to live forever—*somewhere.* This means that there is plenty of time to get things right again if they have gone wrong. No matter what unpleasant thing has happened, prayer can set it right sooner or later. No matter what your difficulty may be it is only a question of enough prayer, and that difficulty will dissolve. No matter what mistake you may have made, enough prayer will overtake it and cancel it—so why worry? If those you love seem to be acting foolishly, you can help them with prayer to be wiser, and, meanwhile, if they suffer, it means that kindly nature is teaching them a lesson that they need to learn. When they have learned that lesson, they will quit, and behave rightly—and so forth.

But supposing something awful should happen! Well, *what then?* If it did, God is stronger than anything "awful," and can put things right again as the result of prayer. Suppose you got sick. *What then?* God can heal you. Suppose you lost everything and landed in the poorhouse. *What then?* Think what a wonderful demonstration you could make out of there and you would probably learn several valuable lessons there, and, anyway, it would be quite interesting. Suppose you lost your heart's delight. *What then?* You cannot lose what really belongs to you. So God will bring it back more wonderful than ever. Suppose the whole universe blew up. *What then?* Let it blow up, and when the dust settles, God will still be in business and you will be alive somewhere, ready to carry on through prayer and understanding. So don't worry.

Remember Lot's Wife

N ever look back. Always go right ahead. Even if you are quaking, go right ahead, and quake as you go. Jesus said the man who puts his hand to the plow and then turns back, is not worthy of the Kingdom of Heaven. He also said: "Remember Lot's wife."

The story of Lot's wife is one of the most telling parables in the Bible. Lot and his family were fleeing from a city that was just about to be destroyed. They were told by an angel that they would get away safely *provided they did not look back*. The others obeyed the injunction and escaped, but Lot's wife looked back—and was immediately turned into a pillar of salt. Salt in the Old Testament is a symbol for death, and this means that those who look back are dead spiritually and that usually their material affairs become stagnant too.

Never look back. No matter how unattractive or how dangerous the road ahead may be, it is better than the road back. The road ahead may mean difficulty, but the road back means failure. The road ahead may be veiled from sight, but you must teach yourself to regard the unknown as friendly.

Remember that God is always at the end of the road ahead, but at the end of the road back you will only find yourself.

The Eternal Incarnation

Christmas is the festival of the rebirth. Sooner or later we all have to be born again as Jesus said, because it is no use trying to patch up the old man. The way of salvation is to let a new man be born. This new birth is brought about by realizing our essential oneness with God, and this is the real meaning of Christmas.

That this can be done, that we can really become the conscious expression of God, is the most wonderful news in the world, and that is why it is called the Gospel.

For the same reason, everyone should be happy at Christmas, and the best way to be happy yourself is to make others happy. *To find the Christ in yourself is to find It in all others too.*

Most people have some extra leisure at Christmas time. This year try the experiment of spending some of that time in definitely seeking the Wonder Child in yourself. Think about it, affirm it, listen for the response. The reason so many people miss the Best Thing in Life is that their hearts are so cluttered up with the intimate details of everyday living that there is no room for the one thing that matters. The Christmas holiday is an ideal time to prepare your soul for the great incarnation. Seek, and you shall find.

True Place and Right Place

T here is a vital difference between your True Place and your Right Place, which everyone should understand.

Your *True* Place is the place where God intends you to be. In that place you will have great happiness, good health, and real prosperity, and you will be living an active and interesting life. That place is waiting for you somewhere, and the wonderful thing about it is that no one but yourself can fill it. Positively no one else on earth but yourself can fill your True Place adequately.

Your *Right* Place in life is the place you are actually in at the moment, whether it is pleasing to you or not.

You are always in your right place because you are always in the place that corresponds to your mentality at the moment, but this may not be your True Place. If your conditions are unwelcome, it means that there is something in your mentality that needs to be changed. Change it, and then the outer conditions will change too.

The sick man is in his Right Place in bed, because he has a sick mentality, but it is not his True Place, and his business is to change his mentality—heal his mind, in fact. When he is healed, bed will no longer be his Right Place. The man in the bread-line has a poverty consciousness at the moment, and suffers the natural consequences, but it is not his True Place, and Scientific Prayer will set him free too. The man in jail is a like case, and so on.

You glorify God by working upon yourself until your Right Place and your True Place become one.

Criticism Versus Discrimination

Personal criticism is one of the dead weights that hold us in limitation. The sole reason why some people do not get their healing, or find their True Place in life, is that they constantly indulge in personal criticism—mental, if not spoken. Here you have an infallible test of your spiritual progress—How fast are you overcoming personal criticism? Unless you are trying to get rid of this you need not expect health, happiness, or freedom.

Now, this does not mean that we are not to exercise discrimination. Wise discrimination is an expression of Divine Intelligence. Of course, we must distinguish between good quality and poor quality everywhere, or where would be the joy of living? We must distinguish good conduct from bad conduct, good music from bad music, wisdom from stupidity, truth from error and, indeed, it is our first duty to do this. We must distinguish truth from error all day long, separating the sheep from the goats, if we are to be true witnesses for God. But this is obviously quite a different thing from personal criticism. Condemn the sin but not the sinner. Deprecate foolish conduct but do not hate the foolish one for it. Rather help him with the right thought. If a singer sings a false note, of course, you must recognize the fact, but do not censure him unkindly. If a friend is doing what you know to be wrong, you cannot condone the wrong, but you can see the Christ in him, and you may even point out the error to him if you are entitled to do so.

Under any circumstances you must keep your own thought poised, tolerant, and kindly. Remember the Golden Rule.

How Much Ocean?

D ivine Mind is infinite and within it are infinite resources—infinite Life, infinite Love, infinite Wisdom, infinite Power, and infinite Substance. The only question is, how much of these things can you appropriate for your use?

How much Intelligence can you assimilate and make use of? How much Understanding can you grasp? How much Divine Love can you experience? How much Divine Substance can you make your own? The supply is inexhaustible; the only limit lies within yourself.

When you go down to the seashore, you find what is practically an unlimited supply of sea water at your disposal. There are billions upon billions of gallons there, but the amount that you can carry away will depend upon the vessel with which you have provided yourself. If you take a ten gallon can, you can get ten gallons, but if you take only a pint pot you can take away only a pint, and if you had nothing bigger than a thimble, you would not be able to take away more than a thimbleful.

So it is with divine abundance. The only limit is the limit of our capacity to receive.

Friday Had Something There

R obinson Crusoe found a primitive savage on his lonely island, and, having made friends with him, he succeeded in teaching him enough of the English language to enable them to exchange ideas. Crusoe being a seventeenth century Englishman, the conversation naturally turned to theology before long, and he surprised and mystified that simple Blackamoor with the far-fetched and illogical doctrines on which he had been brought up.

He told Friday that there is a God who is entirely good and that He has boundless wisdom and infinite power. Friday readily assented to this, but when Crusoe went on to explain that there was also a personal devil who constantly hindered and spoiled God's work, interfered with the scheme of creation, and in many cases even brought about the eternal destruction of God's own children, the thoughtful savage brought him up short. "Why not God kill the devil and fix everything right, if he can do anything?" asked Friday, and to this, needless to say, the theological Crusoe had no answer.

Defoe's masterpiece is really a metaphysical study. Robinson Crusoe is each one of us, and on the solitary island of our own soul we must sooner or later face up to and solve such fundamental problems as this, if we desire peace of mind and the mastery of life.

The truth of course is that evil is but a false belief (terribly real looking and capable of causing us unlimited suffering, while we do believe in it, yet *only belief*), and

111

that the action of God does constantly destroy it and bring about harmony, whenever we pray scientifically by realizing His Glorious Omnipresence. "In Thy Presence is fullness of joy."

Merry-Go-Round

Almost everyone has, at some time or other, taken a ride on a Merry-Go-Round. No fair ground is complete without one even today, and they will probably endure as long as the swings and the coconuts.

Now the remarkable thing about the Merry-Go-Round is this: You climb up on a horse, and off you go. There is a tremendous amount of rattling and vibration, a wonderful sense of movement, and terrific noise and bustle. On, on you go, and, finally, when it comes to rest, you find that you have arrived—exactly at the spot from which you started. All that bustle and movement and excitement—and you have not advanced one inch. You are exactly where you began.

Unfortunately many people conduct their lives in just this manner. They expend any amount of energy, make a good deal of noise, and imagine they are getting somewhere—only to find after all that they are just where they started out. This is what happens when we rely upon will power to solve our problems. There is much noise and movement, but no progress. The man you are at the moment can only go round in the circle of your present problems, no matter how much noise he may make about it. In order to solve your problems you must become a *different* man, and that you can only do by prayer or treatment.

A *different* man cannot have these problems—they do not belong to him.

It is a pity that the lives of so many people should be just a Merry-Go-Round or, rather, what in practice turns out to be a Sad-Go-Round, for such things are not really necessary. If you find yourself the victim of this condition you can break the vicious circle if you will cease to struggle mentally and, instead, turn to God in prayer. *Acquaint thou thyself with Him and be at peace.*

God Must Live in You

Y our own mentality has all power to make your life into anything good or bad. This is the great truth about man. Your own mentality makes your body what it is. If you have a damaged organ, that damage is caused by your own mentality, and if you change your thought about it, it will be healed. If your surroundings are unpleasant, that unpleasantness is caused by your own mentality, and when your mentality changes, the surroundings will change too. If your problem is lack, that lack is caused by your own mentality, and if you change your mentality, prosperity will come.

You are not really affected by other people, or by habit, or climate, or the market, or the administration, or the world situation, or by any other conceivable cause except your own mentality.

Divine Life has to be expressed by Life thoughts in *you* if it is to heal you. Divine Love has to become a sense of love in your *own* heart if it is to heal you—or anyone else by means of you. Divine Intelligence has to become conscious understanding in your mentality if it is to guide and save you. Divine Peace has to be experienced in practice by *you* before it can change your life.

These qualities must be made a part of your *own mentality* before they can affect your life. Thinking of them as merely belonging to an outside God can do nothing for you. Jesus warned us that the Kingdom of God is within.

What Jesus Christ Taught

T he principal points in the Jesus Christ teaching are the Omnipresence and Availability of God, and the belief that because God not only transcends His universe but is everywhere immanent in it—that He indwells in it—it must in reality reflect His perfection. It is prayer that opens the door of the soul so that the Divine Power may work its will to harmony and peace.

Jesus Christ taught that physical ailments are really maladies of the soul outpictured on the body, and that with the healing of the soul accomplished, the healing of the body must follow. The soul is vivified by drawing closer to God through prayer and meditation, and by changing one's outer conduct to bring it more completely in harmony with God's law.

Jesus Christ taught the efficacy of Scientific Prayer to reshape one's whole life for health, harmony, and spiritual development. By Scientific Prayer is meant the Practice of the Presence of God.

Prayer Is the Remedy

*R*emember that the one thing that matters is *prayer.* Time spent in prayer is never wasted. If you do not pray, you cannot expect results.

You may say, "I do not actually pray much, but I keep my thoughts right all day." This is self-deception of a deadly kind. If you were keeping your thoughts right, you would find yourself giving much time to prayer. Pray definitely for yourself every day or you will get nowhere.

If you are fearful, or worried, or tired, or discouraged, or hurried, or disappointed, or in pain, God is your sure remedy—*so pray.*

If you will pray faithfully and regularly and try to live up to the best that you know, it is only a question of time before all troubles, all doubts and fears, all sad memories, all mistakes, will fade away forever, and perfect peace and joy will come into your life.

Spotlights

For heaven's sake, come to the point—and then keep to the point. Don't beat about the bush. Don't go from New York to New Jersey by way of Europe and Australia.

Cultivate a sense of humor. Look for the funny side of everything. It is always there, and will help you to meet any situation. Laugh at yourself at least once before ten o'clock every morning.

You cannot "thumb your way" into heaven; you must work your passage.

Not too much of anything.

If you love your country, don't break her laws.

It is said that the man who can hold his tongue can hold anything.

Radiate happiness, and you help and inspire everyone you meet. Cultivate happiness, and then you must radiate it, for it cannot be concealed. Misery can be hidden, but happiness can no more be kept a secret than garlic can.

Coffee for Three

W e make mental laws for ourselves and then we have to live under them. Unfortunately, it too often happens that these are laws of limitation. We suggest a disability to ourselves, or someone else does it for us, and before we realize what has happened it has become an almost sacred dogma—yet it is only suggestion, and with a change of belief we can be free.

A young doctor and his wife were entertaining a visiting, relative. After dinner coffee was served, whereupon the visitor said excitedly, "John, you know I cannot drink coffee! The nicotine in it keeps me awake all night."

The wife was about to speak but her husband signaled her with his eyes, and said, "I assure you, my dear aunt, there is no nicotine in this coffee." The visitor replied, "There is always nicotine in coffee, and it keeps me awake the whole night." The host then said, "My dear aunt, I assure you upon my word of honor as a doctor, that there is no nicotine in this coffee."

The old lady, who had the highest regard both for her nephew's professional qualifications and for his personal integrity, was satisfied, and thereupon drank three large cups of coffee, enjoyed them immensely—and slept like a top all night.

Naturally, there can be no *nicotine* in coffee; what the old lady meant was *caffeine*, but she said *nicotine*. Of course, one does not approve of the deception employed—deception is never legitimate—but the story illustrates perfectly the power of good and bad suggestion.

The old lady first made a law of limitation for herself, and then repealed it without any trouble.

Why not start today and repeal some of the many such laws you are sure to have made for yourself.

Look Where You Are Going

L ook where you are going, because you will inevitably go where you are looking. Where your attention is, there is your destiny.

Attention is the key to life. Whatever you really give your attention to, you become. Whatever you really concentrate upon will come into your life. We grow into the thing that fills our thoughts as inevitably as the stream merges into the ocean at last.

The Bible says that as a man thinketh *in his heart,* so is he. It does not say simply as a man thinketh, but as he thinketh *in his heart,* and this means *thinking without interest or feeling.*

It has been said that we grow like the thing we admire, but since we are certain to think a good deal about what we really admire, this is only another way of saying that we become the thing to which we give our attention.

This law is often illustrated most amusingly in practical life. The "horsy" man with his equine looks, is known to us all. Kipling speaks of a Newfoundland fisherman who appeared for all the world like a great codfish himself, and Dickens speaks of a pedantic old lawyer who looked just like an animated roll of parchment. Keep your eyes open for these amusing dramatizations, and be sure to take to heart the tremendous lesson that they teach.

He Beat the Cards

From some points of view, the story of your life may very well be compared to a game of cards. In any card game a hand of cards is dealt to you, and it is then up to you to play those cards as you think fit.

Some people receive an excellent hand from the dealer, but they play their cards so foolishly that they lose the game notwithstanding. Another person will receive a very poor hand, but by playing wisely and carefully, finish up by winning the game against all odds.

So it is with the game of life. Some people start out seemingly with every advantage that nature or circumstances can confer, but they play this splendid hand so badly that they wind up in failure and disappointment. Others appear to receive the poorest kind of hand from the Great Dealer—very few trumps—but by the exercise of wisdom, common sense, industry, and, above all, prayer, they play this poor hand so successfully that when the game is over, they have achieved a brilliant and lasting success, and carried off all the "chips" of life.

No matter what sort of hand you may have been dealt, and no matter what mistakes you may have made, the round is not yet over and you may still make a real success of your life, if you will begin today to play your cards scientifically.

Spiritual Jitterbugs

T he best way to study metaphysics is to find the teacher or center that seems to appeal most to you and then concentrate upon that method for a reasonable length of time. If, after such a reasonable period of trial, you decide that that method is not for you, select another one and give that a fair trial in turn, but do not run about from one method to another.

Some people rush around from teacher to teacher and center to center, sometimes going to half a dozen different places in a week, until their minds are in complete chaos. No one gets anywhere through this sort of thing. Such people are not students of metaphysics—*they are spiritual jitterbugs.*

If you were studying voice, for example, and you tried to follow three or four methods at the same time, you know what would happen to your singing, and the study of metaphysics is in many respects comparable to the study of music.

Never forget that you owe no duty to any teacher, any church, any center, or anything else, except to your own Indwelling Christ. It is your sacred duty to leave any teacher (no matter how much you may respect him or her personally) when you find a better one, but while you are working a particular method you will do well to concentrate upon it exclusively.

One Spanking Should Be Enough

G reat souls learn great lessons from small events. We lesser fry should reflect upon this fact, and endeavor to extract from our experience the lesson that it is certain to contain.

Nothing can happen to you unless it finds some kind of correspondence in your own mentality, and it follows from this that every seeming misfortune is but a signal of something wrong within. When something happens to vex or harass you, refuse to be thrown off your balance; analyze the thing dispassionately; find out where you made the mistake, and resolve never to repeat that false step. Charge the present grief to "experience" in your mental books, and consider it well worthwhile for the lesson you have received. In this way you will make continuous and rapid progress toward Peace of Mind and True Place.

Foolish people make the same mistakes over and over again and are punished afresh every time, but for the intelligent student of life, one spanking is usually enough for the same mistake.

Life Is Change

"I see the Angel of God in every change." This is an affirmation that you should have written inside the cover of your pocketbook and also in some prominent place at home where you will often see it. It is one of the keys of a harmonious and progressive life. Especially in these critical times, it will stand out in your life like a lighthouse in a stormy sea. Change is the law of growth, and growth is the law of life. Without change there can be no growth, and without continual growth, life fades out of any form, leaving what we call death.

There is no greater mistake than to be afraid of change, and yet many intelligent people dread it and cling to what is customary and familiar. To be afraid of change is to doubt the providence of God. It is an unintelligent fear of the unknown. If it were not for the blessing of change, men would still be primitive savages living in caves, and you yourself would still be a child mentally and physically, would you not?

Welcome every change that comes into any phase of your life; insist that it is going to turn out for the better—and it will. *See the Angel of God in it,* and that Angel will make all things new.

We Are All One

Christmas is really the festival of human brotherhood. This is the season when we remember our essential unity, the time when old grudges are forgiven and forgotten, the time of family reunions, and the time of remembrance of absent friends.

This essential unity of the human race is a much deeper and more real thing, however, than most people yet suspect. The truth is that in the most literal sense, we are all one. Really there is but one man—generic man—and we are all but expressions of him. In absolute truth, I am you and you are me, for there is but one. My next door neighbor is really myself; the man I pass on the street is me; the hero that I admire is really me; the most degraded criminal is really me, too.

Those who believe in reincarnation have grasped a cosmic truth—but as a rule their understanding of it is still incomplete. What may be called concurrent reincarnation is the final truth on the subject.

One being, the Son of God, is incarnated in about two thousand million separate bodies on the earth, and this adventure we know as the human race—the incarnation of humanity.

Spotlights

od always knows the answer.

God never hurries.

Minutes spent in praying for wisdom will save hours spent in overtaking your mistakes.

Trying to pray, is praying.

The two poles of life are intelligence and love. Unite them in every activity.

Why does not the other fellow demonstrate? That's his business.

Do not expect to begin your treatment with a realization. Be thankful if you get it when the work is done.

Treat the Treatment

S piritual treatment is really knowing the Truth about a given condition. There appears to be something wrong—someone is sick, or there is inharmony, or perhaps lack—but instead of accepting this, you *remind* yourself of the Truth. This *reminding* oneself of the Truth is a very powerful treatment, because in this way we do not try to wrestle with the evil, but we know that it is not there.

The truth about life is that all is perfect, utter, unchanging harmony, because God is the only Presence and the only Power. As a student of metaphysics you know this, and often merely *reminding* yourself of it brings a quick and beautiful demonstration. Of course there are, however, so-called chronic cases in which the student, despite all he can do, seems to make no progress.

I have known some obstinate and long-standing difficulties to be overcome by the following method: Give one final and definite treatment for the difficulty in question by reminding yourself of the Spiritual Truth concerning it, and then do not treat about the problem again but *treat the treatment* whenever you feel inclined to. Do this by claiming that that treatment was a Divine activity and must be successful. Claim that God worked through you when you gave the treatment and that God's work must succeed. Insist that your treatment, being a Divine activity, cannot be hindered by any seeming difficulties or material conditions. Give thanks for its perfect success and mean what you say.

This is "treating the treatment," and you may do this as often as you like. It has none of the disadvantages that are apt to arise from treating the problem itself too often.

Taking the Train to Boston

T rue mental relaxation is just as important as right mental activity. Wise relaxation and wise activity are the balanced poles of all true action. Today most people realize the necessity for learning to relax physically if health is to be maintained, but even students of metaphysics are not always clear on the need for mental relaxation too.

Many people are constantly subjecting their minds to totally unnecessary wear and tear. They rehearse past troubles mentally, and often they even rehearse trouble that they think is likely to happen tomorrow or next week, thereby helping to bring it upon themselves. They indulge in violent mental arguments with absent people. They cross all kinds of bridges mentally hundreds of miles before they reach them.

We speak colloquially of "taking the train" somewhere—and actually many people who ride in trains do *take* the train mentally the whole journey. And that is why so many people are quite worn out when they arrive at their destination. The New Yorker who "takes the train" to Boston in this way, gets in at Grand Central, sits down uneasily (not even relaxing physically), and immediately begins to wonder whether the train will arrive on time. He wonders whether he will be able to find a Red Cap promptly. In imagination he dashes about the platform in Boston looking for a porter. He runs (mentally) up the steps to the street level. If he knows the city, he dashes mentally through the streets to the place of his appointment. Coming back momentarily to the present, he glances at his watch and looks out the window to see how far the train has gotten—and he keeps this up for the four or five hours of the journey.

Many years ago I noticed that when a train arrives in the terminal from a long run, the locomotive men always seem to come off the train looking fresher than most of the passengers, although they have been working and the passengers have not. This, of course, is the explanation. For the engineer and fireman it was only a routine day's work. They did not dream of trying to "take the train" mentally—they let the engine take it. The passengers who were in a mental turmoil most of the time were trying to take the train and suffered the consequences.

It's Hard If You Think It Is

The value that any experience has for us is the value that we put upon it in our thought. A little reflection will show that this is true throughout the whole gamut of human experience. The same unpleasant happening that one man will laugh off and forget, will to another man mean a broken heart followed by death.

A "big" difficulty is what we consider big. To God there are no big and no little demonstrations. Big and little are qualities that lie in our own thought. To heal a dying man seems a big demonstration to us, and to heal a cut finger seems a little demonstration, but to God one is no more difficult than the other.

If we believed that it was as easy to raise the dead as to heal a cold, we could do it as easily. If we believed it was as easy to demonstrate a house as to demonstrate a lead pencil, we should demonstrate a house as easily as a pencil.

Minimize the problem you are treating. Do not give it importance in your thought. Do not try too hard. A positive, constructive, don't-care feeling is very valuable. And the less hurry you are in for your demonstration, the sooner it will come. If you feel you can wait a year, it will probably come next week. If you can feel that you know it will come and you don't care when, it will probably come tomorrow.

Hurry and pressure are fetters that we place upon our own souls.

The Springtime of the Soul

E aster is the great festival for the celebration of springtime. Ever since men have been on the earth they have marked the coming of spring in some special way. It was natural that they should do this because they have always felt intuitively that the real springtime is the springtime of the soul, and the springtime of the soul is its awakening to God.

Easter, if it has any true significance for us, must mean just this—that the winter of separation and limitation is over. It must mean that now we know who we really are— the children of God—and what our real destiny is— reunion with Him.

The True Easter

Easter when properly understood, symbolizes the supreme spiritual experience, which is the regeneration of mankind. We were not meant to be forever in limitation, fear, and misunderstanding. The design of Providence is that we should awaken to our true spiritual nature, cast off the works of darkness, and go forth clad in the shining armor of light. That is the true Easter.

Jesus passed through the dark night of Calvary to the glorious resurrection of Easter day. The world today is going through a Calvary from which it will emerge purified, strengthened, inspired, in a real Eastertide for the race as a whole.

Individually, each one of us must aim at making the same demonstration for himself by studying the science that Jesus taught and applying it unswervingly in his own life.

Thou Canst Not Steal

S ome people talk as though you could do anything you want to, while others seem to think that you are a puppet of destiny with no choice at all. They are both wrong. The truth is that you can do anything, have anything, be anything, for which you have the consciousness—but not otherwise.

To be healthy you must have a health consciousness. To be prosperous you must have a prosperity consciousness. To be successful in any field of endeavor you must have the consciousness that corresponds.

There is a slang expression that says that to accomplish anything difficult "you must have what it takes." Well, what it "takes" is the consciousness to correspond to it.

We have free will to develop a given kind of consciousness and then we can be and do anything in accordance with that, but *we have no free will to do anything without the consciousness that belongs to that accomplishment.*

To try to get something without having the consciousness to which it belongs is really mental theft, and that, of course, cannot succeed: thou shalt not steal—which really means *thou canst not steal.*

Build up the consciousness for what you truly want and nothing can prevent your having it.

Never Say Die

N ever "write off" a treatment. Never admit to yourself that a treatment has failed. When the demonstration does not come, it means either that you have not done enough work or that for some reason the time is not ripe for that condition to change.

If you feel that you have treated enough, or at least done all that you can, affirm divine harmony and forget it—but do not write it off. I have picked up demonstrations a year after giving the last treatment concerning them, but I had not written them off.

Of course, there is no one policy that will fit every problem. If your common sense does not suggest how a particular problem should be handled, treat for guidance and it will surely come. Concerning matters that are not urgent, it is an excellent practice to give one treatment and leave it—to send up a kite and cut the string.

Your treatment will be just as effective as you think it will be. What you bind in your real belief will be bound, and what you loose with the same conviction will be loosed.

Yes, I Believe It

What do you really believe? This is a vital question, because it is your real belief that determines your destiny. It is as a man thinketh in his *heart* that matters, says the Bible, and this means the heart-felt conviction as distinct from mere formal assent.

If you want to know what you really believe, you can easily find out. Simply watch what you *do*. We always *do* what we believe, although we frequently talk differently.

Therefore watch what you do and this will give you a clue to your real beliefs.

If your conditions are not to your liking, if you feel that you are not making the most of your life, *change your beliefs*. Your present beliefs must be wrong if they are not producing harmony and satisfaction, so change them, and results will be changed too.

Start believing in health, and keep it up. Start believing in prosperity, and keep it up. Start believing in the Christ in those about you, and keep it up. Start believing that your own Divine Selfhood is rapidly unfolding, and keep it up.

Believe these things in your very heart, and act as though you believed them, and the results will surprise you.

Love Acts the Part

P eople are to be judged by their actions. It is futile to say that you feel one thing if you act something else. We sometimes hear it said, "his conduct is bad but at heart he means well"; but this is nonsense because our considered conduct always expresses the sentiments of the heart. In the old-fashioned phrase: *"handsome is as handsome does."*

The bad-tempered person cannot possibly have "a heart of gold" as is sometimes charitably said. A bad-tempered person has a mean, selfish heart and should get busy and change it without delay.

Love acts the part. The man who is unkind to his wife does not love her, in spite of anything he may say. The father who neglects his children does not love them, in spite of any hypocrisy he may indulge in. The man who talks or acts unpatriotically does not love his country even though he waves the flag.

He who loves does not seek his own advantage. He could not seek to hurt or tarnish the one he loved. He could never forget or overlook his duties or obligations. He could not cause suffering or injury to the one he professed to love.

Love acts the part, and anything else is hypocrisy.

A Way of Life

T rue Christianity is a life to be lived, not just a set of intellectual theories to be accepted. It is a Way of Life, and that means that your religion must function all day long.

Particular demonstrations are important because they prove the Law, but all particular demonstrations are secondary to the practical conduct of life. A good healer can lift you over a certain stile by removing from your consciousness the effects of past wrong thinking—but unless you cease to think wrongly upon that subject the trouble will return.

I once had a long talk with the late Mr. Sandow, the famous "strong man," in his palatial gymnasium in London. He said, "People come to me with a blank check in their hands and say, 'I will pay you any fee you like if you will produce for me a strong, healthy, young body,' I say, 'Excellent'—but then it turns out that I am to go into the gymnasium and swing dumbbells and do exercises on the floor, while they go away and eat and drink and smoke too much and keep late hours. Regretfully I tell them, 'It cannot be done.'"

Of course, Sandow was right, and it is with the training of the soul as with the training of the body; in the long run we have to do our own work, and we have to live the right mental life—not sometimes, but all the time.

Spotlights

 A lways pray gently. Work as gently as you would work if you were painting a picture on a cobweb.

To get the right mental attitude and maintain it, even for a few days, will work a revolution in your life.

Your life is conditioned by your own thoughts, not by the thoughts of anyone else.

You cannot change your type, but you can make yourself a brilliant success in that type.

Without some degree of spiritual understanding, there is no real security.

Stoicism is imposed from without by will power; serenity grows from the inside outward.

The root of all our difficulties is a lack of the sense of the Presence of God.

Fletcherize Life!

H orace Fletcher taught people to eat slowly. He said that most of us never enjoy our food because we bolt one course to get to the next and that the meal is over before we begin to taste it.

I have often thought that most of us make this mistake about life in general. Our attention is apt to be so fixed upon tomorrow or next week that we forget to relish this day. People are always going to be happy a little later on when they have done something else first. They are really going to enjoy life when they get a job, or when they retire from business; or when they are married, or when they get a divorce; or when they move into the country, or when they can settle in town; or when they have passed an examination; or when the children are off their hands; or anything else in the whole world.

All this is wrong. By all means make your plans and take the right means to carry them out, but meanwhile enjoy each hour of the day as it passes. Ponder the wonderful old saying that *tomorrow never comes*. Enjoy the living of today while today is here. There are all sorts of interesting things happening in everyone's life every day. They may be small things, but they are nevertheless worthwhile.

When visiting several rather primitive Central American countries, I was greatly struck by the fact that these simple people, whose ways of life are very elementary, and who are almost without material possessions, nevertheless seem to get much more out of life than do many of our own relatively sophisticated people. Their secret is that they live much more in the present moment than we do. They enjoy life while it is with them. They obviously relish performing the simplest tasks that we rush through almost mechanically. Most of our people seem to be, mentally, always en route to somewhere else or something else.

Of course we have many things of great value that they still lack, but it seems that in our very rapid progress we have forgotten certain important values that these primitive people still retain.

Live in the present moment and find your interest and your happiness in the things of today.

But . . .

The devil is always up-to-date. He is always disguising himself in some new form. Of course, what we call the devil is really just a dramatic name for one's own lower self, that old self (Paul calls it the old Adam) that hates to change, the old self that is lazy and selfish and fearful.

When the devil has been unmasked a number of times, his final refuge seems to be the harmless looking word *but*.

Students of the Jesus Christ teaching who would not be deceived by any of the familiar devices, constantly surrender their principles, and therefore their demonstration, to the little word *but*.

They say, "Of course I know that God is the only power—*but*. . . ." Or,

"Of course I know that God is omnipresent, and so He must really be where I see this problem— *but*...." Or,

"Of course I know that God is love, so there can be nothing to be afraid of—*but*...." Or,

"Of course I know that there is no hurry because I am in eternity—*but*. . . ." Or,

"Of course I know that John or Mary must be the living expression of God, as I am—*but*. . . ." Or,

And this little word *but* destroys the whole treatment and prevents the action of God from taking place at that particular point. By that one word they have denied God.

If Truth is true, there are no *buts*, and, of course, we know that the Bible is right and that divine harmony is a fact.

Know the Truth (without qualification) and the Truth will set you free.

143

Let's Not Be Cocksure

Have you an open mind? Is the window of your soul open for fresh air and the sunshine of Truth to come in, or is it closed and shuttered by mental laziness or the emotional congestion that we call prejudice?

None of us knows how many fine things we have missed through being self-satisfied and cocksure. I do not think that anyone can be considered really intelligent who does not have a sense of balance and proportion, some sense of the value of evidence, and *a readiness to examine new ideas* with an open mind.

The history of scientific discovery shows that almost every new step was opposed by the very people who should have welcomed it.

Harvey was denounced for claiming that the blood circulates through the body instead of standing still, as was believed at the time. Galileo was persecuted for saying that the earth went round the sun, and "learned" men refused even to look through his telescope. Pasteur was branded a quack by his professional colleagues for advancing the germ theory of disease—the theory for which most scientists would be willing to go to the stake today. Jenner was threatened with the police for pioneering vaccination—and by the very medical bodies who swear by it now. The finality of the atom, which was a scientific dogma in the childhood of most of us, has been completely discarded by the same scientific pundits today.

Many of the Truths put forward by the New Thought movement years and years ago are gradually being accepted by academic science, which at first laughed them to scorn.

Right now you can sit in your home in New York and listen to the voice of a man talking in Paris, or a woman singing in London, and it was only a very short time ago that such a feat would have seemed quite impossible—a few generations ago the people who did it would have stood in serious danger of being hanged or even burned alive for witchcraft.

Probably the only incorrigible fool is the man who says that anything is impossible, that everything has been done, or that there is any limit to the conquests that Divine Intelligence working in mankind can achieve.

The truth is that nothing that is good is impossible.

Don't Be a Dinosaur

In a certain museum in New York they have a couple of dinosaur's eggs on view. This exhibit is very popular with the public because it appeals to the imagination. Visitors say, "Isn't it interesting. She laid those eggs millions of years ago, and here they are today untouched!"

Interesting to us they undoubtedly are, but thoughtless people are apt to overlook the fact that for the dinosaur in question they represent just complete failure. After all the trouble of laying those eggs nothing ever came of them—wasted effort.

It is surprising how many otherwise intelligent men and women waste the best days of their lives laying dinosaur's eggs that they never hatch out. Either through lack of energy, or lack of intelligent planning, or failure to make God a partner, or more often sheer muddle-headedness, they lay an excellent egg and then stroll away and forget it.

Don't be a dinosaur. Do not start a plan unless you really think it is worthwhile, and if you are convinced that it is worthwhile, do not rest until you have brought it to fruition. Jesus had something to say about those who put their hand to the plow and then look back.*

Select something worth doing; take God for your partner in the enterprise, and keep at it until success is assured. *Don't be a dinosaur.*

*Luke 9:62.

146

Spiritual Sunbathing

I n many cases the best form of prayer is just to think about God and His Presence with you. This quiet contemplation of God is simply to enjoy the Presence without attempting, so to speak, to do anything with it.

Particularly, if you are emotionally disturbed about something, or when you are worried about a number of different problems, this gentle but persistent preoccupation with the great Creative Mind will restore your inner peace and open the way to victory.

We need to learn to relax spiritually as well as physically. We easily forget that it is the power of God that solves our problem and not our own efforts in the making of our prayers. Sunbathing offers an excellent analogy here. In sunbathing you expose the skin to the solar rays, and then you relax and leave it to the sun to do the rest. You would never think of trying to help the sun. You would never think of trying to rub the sunbeams into your skin, nor would you strain upward in an endeavor to get nearer to the sun, for instance. You relax quietly and have perfect faith that the sun will do its work.

In meditating on the Presence of God the same quiet relaxed confident attitude will bring the same inevitable result.

Fools' Gold

I n mining country one comes across a valueless substance that is so like gold ore that inexperienced people cannot always tell the difference. This is called fools' gold, and many a young prospector has wasted much time and hard work before discovering that he has been deceived by the spurious article.

Old miners used to say to the tenderfoot: "When you think you have found gold you probably have not, but when you do find it, you will know it for certain."

So it is with prospectors on the mountain range that we call life. Here there are many kinds of fools' gold to be found, but when you meet the genuine article you will have no doubt in your mind. The true gold will give you a sense of peace and poise that nothing belonging to this world can furnish. It will give you a sense of freedom and power because you will no longer be in bondage to passing material things. It will set you free from much of the tyranny of the time and space beliefs.

Fools' gold usually takes the form of material riches, social prominence, power over others, physical enjoyment, and so forth. The true gold is that sense of the Presence of God with us, to obtain which is the object of this life.

Now You Must Do It

The only part of our religion that is real is the part we express in our daily lives. Ideals that we do not act out in practice are mere abstract theories and have no real meaning. Actually, such pretended ideals are a serious detriment, because they drug the soul into a false sense of security.

If you want to receive any benefit from your religion you must practice it, and the place to practice it is right here where you are, and the time to do it is *now.*

Divine Love is the only real power. If you can realize this fact even dimly it will begin to heal and harmonize every condition in your life within a few hours. The way to realize this fact is to express it in every word you speak, in every business transaction, in every social activity, and, in fact, in every phase of your life.

An early New Thought writer said: "Knead love into the bread you bake; wrap strength and courage in the parcel you tie for the woman with the weary face; hand trust and candor with the coin you pay to the man with the suspicious eyes." This is beautifully said, and it sums up the Practice of the Presence of God.

To Him That Hath

*For unto every one that hath shall be given, and he shall
have abundance: but from him that hath not shall be taken
away even that which he hath.*

—MATTHEW 25:29

T his great text has been a stumbling-block to many. It looks like injustice. It sounds like cruelty. Yet Jesus said it, and we know that he was always right and that he taught that we reap as we sow.

The explanation is perfectly simple and logical when you have the metaphysical key to life. Your experience is the outpicturing or expression (pressing out) of your state of mind or consciousness, at any time. When your consciousness is high or relatively good, everything goes well. When your consciousness is relatively low or limited, everything goes wrong.

Trouble comes because the consciousness has fallen a little. The usual thing then is to meet the trouble with fear, anger, disappointment, self-pity, or brutal will power. This naturally lowers the consciousness a good deal more, and things get still worse—and so on. From him that hath not (much) harmony, shall be taken away even that which he hath.

Harmony and joy come into your life because your mental state is comparatively high. This happiness naturally raises your consciousness and your faith in God still higher, and so things improve further. Unto everyone that hath shall be given, and he shall have abundance.

150

All this is a simple statement of natural law, and to understand and apply this law will bring you out of any difficulty into harmony and true success. What seemed at first to be unjust and cruel turns out to be a trumpet call of courage and hope.

The proverb, "It never rains but it pours," is another way of stating the same law.

Let us thank God that this wonderful law exists.

Rossini Slept It Away

A delightful story is told about Rossini, the famous composer. It seems that the first night that his opera, *The Barber of Seville*, was produced, it was very badly received. Hisses and cries of derision followed the fall of the curtain. No such scene had occurred in the memory of anyone present. The prima donna was in hysterics. The leading man darkly talked of suicide. Then they looked for the composer, but he was nowhere to be found.

"The worst has happened," cried the distraught manager. "The maestro has destroyed himself." They all rushed off in a body to Rossini's lodgings and discovered him sound asleep in bed. They woke him up. They cried, "Maestro, are you all right?" Rossini replied, "I was having a nice sleep before you woke me." They said, "But the opera! The fiasco!"

Rossini replied, "Evidently *The Barber* is not good enough, so I must compose something better, that is all. But we will discuss that in the morning. Now please let me sleep." And he relapsed into slumber.

As everyone knows, *The Barber* turned out to be an immense success, and has played steadily for over a hundred years, being received with enthusiasm in New York only last season.

We see from this that Rossini was a great philosopher as well as a great composer. Without knowing it, he was practicing New Thought. This story is a perfect example of how we should meet seeming failure and difficulty in order to turn it into success.

Your Mind Is Your Laboratory

Y ou have probably visited a chemical or electrical laboratory at some time or other, even if you have not done any scientific work yourself. You saw the scientist busy with retorts, test tubes, thermometers, voltmeters, or ammeters. He weighed and measured carefully, checked his readings, increased or decreased pressures, and so forth, never acting at random or trusting to luck. The result of this policy has, of course, been the unparalleled triumphs of modern science in its own field—the efficient automobile, the priceless electric light, the incredible radio, the age-old dream of man in flight, and, perhaps most wonderful of all, the familiar telephone. *The scientific method has justified itself.* In Christian metaphysics we learn that man's mentality is his scientific laboratory— just that. In your daily thinking and reading and talking, you are handling the retorts and test tubes and ammeters of the mental world. To handle them correctly, like a scientist, is to produce practical results comparable to his. This means to have health, harmony, and true success in your life.

To be negative, inconsistent, and slovenly in your mental life is to ensure trouble and failure.

The negative things in your mind—the fears, doubts, resentments—are to be starved out of existence by refusing to feed them with the attention upon which they live. The positive Christ things are to be nourished by thoughts of Divine Love, harmony, peace, and the Practice of the Presence of God. This work is to be done systematically and consistently in the spirit of the scientific chemist, for results always reflect the methods behind them.

To him that hath shall be given; so, see that what you have is a consciousness of harmony and peace. From him that hath not shall be taken away even that which he hath; so, see to it that you have very little negative thinking in your life, and then even what you have will be taken away and your corresponding limitations will follow it.

We reap as we sow.

Sensitive But Happy

To be sensitive is good, because sensitive people are aware of a thousand interesting or beautiful things where the obtuse person gets nothing. If our thick-skinned friends avoid a lot of suffering, they also miss the finest things in life.

To do any creative work you have to be sensitive, because the creative worker is a "receiving set" for Divine Mind. The sensitiveness of the artist is proverbial. A world famous tenor, who was literally fretting himself to death over unimportant matters, broke down in my office and said that God was cruel to make him so sensitive. I replied, "If you had the hide of a rhinoceros you might be a happier man, but you would not be at the Metropolitan."

Many people, however, are too sensitive. They respond to all kinds of unpleasant vibrations that do not concern them. We can train ourselves to reduce this sort of thing to a minimum, but we should be careful to see that we shut out negative things only and still leave ourselves open to the True, the Beautiful, and the Good. Here is an affirmation that, intelligently used, will save you much unnecessary bombardment by negative thoughts: *I am positive to everything but the action of God.*

In an electric circuit any given point is said to be positive to any point below it and negative to any point above it. Current passes always from the positive to the negative and never the other way. Now, if you are positive in this sense to everything but the action of God, no negative things can come back at you. On the other hand, you are receptive (or "negative" in the purely electrical sense of this ambiguous word) to all good—the direct inspiration of God, the prayers of other people, and all the beautiful and interesting vibrations in the universe,

The first two or three metaphysical meetings I ever conducted left me with a feeling of fatigue and depression. On thinking it over I realized that I had been leaving myself open to all the mental conflicts in the audience, and by using the above affirmation I overcame this problem in a few days.

The sword of the spirit is the Word of God.

Your Criminal Ear

Many years ago a foolish professor wrote a book in which he said that he could always tell if a person were a potential criminal by the shape of his ear!

This naturally created something of a furor, and a London newspaper sent a reporter to interview old General Booth, of the Salvation Army, on the subject.

He said, "General, you probably have an unmatched experience of human nature in the raw. Do you believe there is such a thing as a criminal ear?"

William Booth laughed loudly through his Mosaic beard, and replied, "Why, of course there is a 'criminal ear'—*and we've all got one.* If it were not for the grace of God, every one of us would be doing time or deserving to."

William Booth understood human nature. You never can afford to condemn another, because in his shoes you would probably have done just as badly or worse. You never know to what temptation another person has been subjected. You cannot tell how much ignorance or sheer stupidity has had to do with his fault. You should thank God that you know better (if you really do) and help him with the right thought, instead of pushing him still farther down mentally. Have you not noticed that sometimes after condemning someone else rather pharasaically, you have shortly afterward caught yourself committing the very same fault?

Wisely did the Master say: *Judge not.*

Express the thing that you want to be—this is a good rule in metaphysics. Act the part you really want to play. If you want to be a hero, act heroically in the plain things of everyday life, even if it involves a good deal of sacrifice—as it will. If you want to be a saint, lead a saintly life here and now; there is no other way. If you want to know God, keep company with Him. The only way to get to know a human being is to spend time in his company, and the same is true of God.

If you want prosperity, think only prosperity thoughts, speak only prosperity words, and as far as your means allow, act out the part too. A penny-pinching policy in money matters gradually builds a penny-poor consciousness.

This is unchangeable metaphysical law; but remember that the law must be obeyed if the law is to act. You must really *pay the price*, for you cannot fool the Law. To be a hero you *must* be heroic. For spiritual mastership you *must* walk with God.

Some people, in the name of metaphysics, try to shunt their responsibilities onto someone else's shoulders, but while they may fool themselves in this way, they cannot fool the Law.

A woman came to me in distress about money. It appeared that she had a charge account at Wanamaker's and had ordered a dress that had been duly delivered and worn by her, although she had no money left. It was the third of the month and the bill had arrived the day before. I said, "Why did you order a dress, not having the money to pay for it?" She replied, "I believe in stepping out on God." I said, "That was not stepping out on God; that was stepping out on Wanamaker. It was unjust and dishonest." She wept. I told her that tears would not help either her or her creditor. She was sorry for herself; I was sorry for the department store and told her so. Finally, her sister, who could not really afford it, gave her the money. But she had learned her lesson and is now demonstrating finance very comfortably.

If you are going to work with God you must work in the Spirit of God, and you must not count the cost. Casting the burden on other people is only selfishness and evasion. You step out on God when you build yourself a true God consciousness, and that will never penalize anyone else.

In the Beginning, Me

T he first four words of the Bible are *in the beginning, God*. This fact is very significant because it indicates that God must be the beginning of anything worthwhile. Here it begins the Bible, and the text goes on to deal with the creation of the universe, showing that God, of course, is the real beginning of all things.

If you take this thought *in the beginning, God*, and make it the keynote of your whole life, you have found the secret of success. If you make this principle the keynote of any particular enterprise, that enterprise must and will be successful.

The trouble with so many people is that the actual keynote of their lives is *in the beginning, me*. They are not always aware of this. As a rule they do not even suspect it, but the fact remains.

The real cause for the inharmony in the world is that so many individuals, groups, and nations think in terms of *in the beginning, me*.

Working from yourself as the center can only bring discouragement, depression, and failure. Working from God as the center, not nominally but actually, must bring success, for God is Creative Life.

The Bible says, "I am Alpha and Omega, the beginning and the end"—the First and the Last. This means that where God is the beginning you will find He is also the end, that your demonstration will be complete, perfect, and final.

Can't-Be-Done's

Here is a wonderful saying: "He didn't know that it couldn't be done, so he did it." Meditate upon this, and you will find it very inspiring.

It is amazing to think how many interesting and worthwhile things most of us could do, if we had not put mental handcuffs on ourselves. What happens to many people is this: When they are young they are full of ambition and confidence, and they attempt to do a number of interesting things. Being young, they lack experience, or the necessary means to accomplish their desires, and, after a number of failures, they become permanently discouraged and decide that after all they cannot do anything worthwhile. Also they unwisely discuss their plans with other people, who thoughtlessly discourage or even snub them. Thus it is that the lives of most grown-up people are full of *can't-be-done's*. They say "I can't do this," and "I can't do that," and "I am never able to do such a thing," and "of course something else is impossible for me." Often they have a spurious reason—"my health," "my constitution," "my early training" (or lack of it). "My age" is a favorite excuse for laziness. "My family" is a pretty good excuse too, and, of course, there are always the climate, the unfavorable locality, and the depression.

A great industrialist has a rule in his works that when his research department fails to solve a problem, no records of these experiments are kept. He says that these failures would be accepted as final and would prevent new men from ultimately solving those problems. He is right, of course, in thus repudiating *can't-be-done's*.

Have a mental stock-taking and ruthlessly throw out all the *can't-be-done's* you find in yourself. Break those handcuffs with the power of Truth. Just as you are today, you can do some wonderful things for yourself and those you love *if you will get rid of the can't-be-done's*.

Change Your Mind—
And Keep It Changed

I f some condition in your life is not to your liking, *change your mind about it—and keep it changed*. If someone is displeasing to you, change your mind about him—and keep it changed. If there is some sad memory that haunts you, change your mind about it—and keep it changed.

Most students of metaphysics are ready to change their minds about a problem, especially when they have just been to a lecture or talked with a teacher, but they *do not keep them changed*.

This is the crux of the matter. If you will change your mind concerning anything and *absolutely keep it changed*, that thing must and will change too. It is the keeping up of the change in thought that is difficult. It calls for vigilance and determination. But surely it is worthwhile, seeing that it is the key to Dominion.

Make an experiment now. Change your mind concerning some particular thing in your life and *keep it changed*, and I guarantee that you will be amazed and delighted at the result.

Too Old at Something

One of the imaginary bogeys that spoil people's lives is the idea of being too old. This bogey is an imaginary one, but nevertheless it can ruin everything, as long as you believe in it.

Before the last war someone created the stupid slogan, "Too old at forty," and many people picked it up and used it to cripple their lives. People of twenty have told me they were too old to do something that, in reality, they would not be ready for under another ten years. And once a child of fifteen said to me he supposed he was too old to do something or other that he wanted to do.

For practical purposes you are as old or as young as your consciousness—as old or as young as your real belief. This is not just theory but admits of practical proof, and many people have proved it.

Of course, it is in seeking employment that the too-old-to-do-something bogey is most troublesome. People say, "What is the use of looking for work when the first question they ask is about my age?" Now the truth is that if you feel that way about your age it will indeed be a stumbling block, but *it is you who make it so.* You believe in your heart that your age is a handicap. This thought and the great fear that goes with it are uppermost in your mind. The man who would engage you gets this from you and immediately asks about your age. He is responding to your own thought.

But, if you will work on yourself until you have really risen above this fear—until you really do feel that your age does not matter—the prospective employer either will not ask about your age at all or he will not care about it. Where a form has to be filled out, he will either not notice your age or not care.

A number of people, in what is sometimes called later life, have proved this law to their great advantage.

Too-old-to-do-something is a purely personal bogey and has no existence outside of your own mind.

You are as old as eternity and as young as God, and others will put the valuation on your age that you really put on it yourself.

Is That Your Hat?

Why has not your prayer been answered? Perhaps it has. Strangely enough, it often happens that we receive an answer to our prayer and do not recognize it. Some of us have had demonstrations in our possession for weeks or months and have not known it. This mistake is caused by outlining. We have unconsciously decided that the demonstration must take a particular form, and because that form does not appear, we think we have failed. Actually we probably have an even better demonstration than we expected, but for the moment we are blind to it.

If a boy prayed for a man's hat (because he thought it would look well on him or make him grown up) he would not get it because Divine Wisdom knows that he could not wear it. He would get a good hat of the sort that would be useful to him. We often pray for things for which we are not really prepared, but if we pray scientifically this will not matter, since Creative Intelligence will send us the thing that we really need.

The Practice of the Presence of God is the perfect prayer because it understands everything and overlooks nothing.

Seek God for His own sake, *for the joy of being with Him,* and demonstrations will take care of themselves.

I Bless Him—He's a Devil

I recently received a letter from a man with a business problem. He was having trouble with two men who, he said, were trying to swindle him out of a large sum of money by misrepresenting the terms of an agreement. He said:

"I have been a student of metaphysics for many years, and for a week past I have spent some time every morning realizing the Christ in each of these men and knowing that they are the perfect children of God and must express truth and wisdom; for that is the Law of Being. They are a most unscrupulous pair and are notorious in our city for their underhanded dealings, and one of them came near going to jail some time ago. They are financial sharks of the lowest type. I continue to realize the Divine Presence in them, and I am writing to ask you to speak the Word for me."

This appalling letter throws a searchlight on the mistake that keeps so many people from demonstrating. This man spent time each morning trying to realize the Christ in his "enemies," then went on, even in his letter, to think evil of them, and seemed to imagine that finishing with a well-sounding phrase would undo all this harm.

It is obvious that what he really felt about them was evil and that the good he voiced was merely a pious formality. In order to demonstrate, he would have to feel the Truth so strongly that the error picture naturally faded out of his consciousness, and so I told him in no uncertain words.

Shrapnel

The Jesus Christ teaching is a passport to peace of mind and steady spiritual progress. Jesus said that if we followed his teachings, nothing would by any means hurt us—and that is true. It usually happens, however, that when we are on the spiritual path, difficulties present themselves from time to time, but as long as they are met with Truth, in the right way, they soon fade out into nothingness, leaving us with a definite spiritual uplift.

Sometimes these difficulties are caused by mistakes we are making at the present time, and such mistakes must be recognized and corrected. But more often they are old negative things working their way out of the subconscious, much as shrapnel works its way out of a living body.

I know a man who was badly wounded in the last war. He is able to earn his living now, but every few weeks a curious thing happens. He will feel a slight itching somewhere on his skin. The following day a tiny lump makes its appearance. Then, a day later, the skin is punctured by a little steel point, and within a few hours another piece of shrapnel has emerged! Of a somewhat morbid temperament, he keeps these gruesome souvenirs in a glass tumbler on the mantlepiece.

The subconscious mind has many fears, doubts, and frustrations buried in its depths, and the sooner they come to the surface, the sooner we shall attain our goal. And so their emergence shrapnel-like into the light of day is all to the good. Meet the problems, worries, and annoyances of daily life in the knowledge that they furnish an opportunity to clear up the subconscious mind very rapidly, and you will be surprised to find how little power they have to impede you. They are shrapnel coming out.

Your Own Valuation

T he world will take you at your own valuation. Your body will take you at your own valuation. Your business will take you at your own valuation, for your own value is the value that you *really* put upon yourself.

"Oh, but," you may say, "that cannot be true, because I know several people who are always boasting and pretending and yet no one ever takes them seriously."

Please note that I said the value you *really* put upon yourself. That important word makes all the difference in the world. People who boast, bluff, and pretend have *really* a poor opinion of themselves—or why would they pretend? And it is this poor opinion or sense of inferiority that is demonstrated in the failure that such people always make of their lives.

The man who really believes that his wares are excellent does not dream of lying about them. The man who is satisfied with what he is, has no incentive to pretend to be something he is not. The man who is conscious of substantial achievement has no desire to boast.

Nature always takes you at your own valuation. Believe you are the child of God—*really* believe it. Believe that you express Divine Life, Divine Truth, and Divine Love. Believe that Divine Wisdom guides you. Believe that God is your supply. Believe that God is helping and blessing humanity through you. Believe that you are a special enterprise on the part of God and that He is opening your way—and what you really believe, that you will demonstrate.

The Glory of His Presence

T he glory of God sweeps into the human soul on the wings of the morning. It is like a summer sunrise, stilling the soul, enlightening the intellect, filling the heart with an ineffable joy.

This glory comes not by accident or by favor. If you really wish for that communion with God that has been the goal of religious men and women in all ages, you must come out for it definitely, and you must discard everything that can possibly retard you upon the journey.

You must set aside a definite time every day for prayer and meditation and for checking up on your own daily conduct, both in external and internal things. You must conduct the affairs of your soul in a businesslike way. Too many religious people fail to realize that the business of spiritual growth calls for order, method, and intelligent organization—just as much as does any commercial business or any engineering enterprise or any other important activity, if it is to be a success—and that, above all, it requires whole-hearted and unwavering devotion and self consecration. *If . . . thou shalt seek the Lord thy God, thou shalt find him, if thou seek him with all thy heart and with all thy soul.**

*Deuteronomy 4:29.

Where's the Fire?

What are you rushing about for, might one ask in a friendly way. Why did you dash out of the house this morning as if a tiger were after you? Why have you been racing about all day like a neurotic grasshopper? Why do you charge along subway platforms like cavalry? What is the idea of writhing with impatience when you do not hear the telephone girl's voice inside of three seconds? Why do you sometimes finish people's sentences for them and "take the words out of their mouths"? Why do you risk your neck dashing into the street thirty seconds before the green light makes it safe?

What is it all about? You appear to be going somewhere—but where? Surely all this frenzied rushing should have a logical objective—but has it?

Actually, I think you will find that it has not. I think if you analyze your movements for one whole day you will discover that three-quarters of your activities have really been wasted motion. You could have done a better day's work with much more profit to yourself and others with about 25 percent of the energy, quietly and scientifically applied— besides going to bed with healthy fatigue instead of nervous prostration.

Where are you going? Well, I do not know about you, but I do know exactly where most people are going—to the cemetery. We know that unless we regenerate we shall die some day. Now people who are regenerating do not rush, because part of the regeneration treatment is to cultivate poise, calm, and patience. So all the rushing and dashing and trampling on other people is just in order to get—to the cemetery. Hardly seems worth it, does it?

Walk along any busy street and study the rushing, surging throng, and note that they are all rushing somewhere—to the graveyard. Of course, the route will be a circuitous one, they will loop round thousands of miles first—but that is the goal to which they are *rushing*.

At the entrance to a large cemetery near New York a notice says, with unconscious irony, "one way traffic only."

Now, is it good enough to wear yourself out, undermine your health, and worry all the joy out of your life just to go off and be buried?

Take it easy. Enjoy life reasonably as you go along. You are really in eternity now, and in eternity no wise man hurries. God does not want us to die. It is we who kill ourselves with hurry and worry. If we understood God's laws and applied them, we could live very long lives on this earth in strong vigorous health, and then, when there was no more to learn here, transcend consciously. Some day the race will learn this. Meanwhile take it easy and trust in God.

Paderewski!—That's Different!

A n amusing story was told to me by the manager of a New York hotel. The great Paderewski occupied a suite there a number of years ago during one of his seasons at Carnegie Hall.

It was the master's custom to practice for a couple of hours every morning on the magnificent instrument that he had brought with him.

On the third morning of his stay an angry lady stormed into the manager's office and said, "Someone is hammering on an old tin can piano every morning across the corridor from me. This is the third day. It is driving me mad, and unless you stop it I shall leave immediately."

The astonished manager remonstrated, "But madam, that is Paderewski himself!"

The lady nearly fainted with surprise and said, "Paderewski! Oh, that's different. Of course I had not the slightest idea. I adore good music. I am an excellent musician myself. Please say nothing at all about it." The hotel man was much amused to note that thereafter, for the remainder of Paderewski's stay, the good woman kept the door of her apartment wide open and entertained a party of friends there every morning while he practiced.

Learn to appreciate the true worth of things. Do not admire things just because other people do, or because such an attitude is considered "correct." Know what you really like. Know what you really want. Be honest with yourself. It may be that your taste in certain directions

174

needs to be improved, but, if so, set out to improve it
honestly and without self-deception. If the opera bores
you, do not go to the Metropolitan just because it is fash-
ionable to do so. If, on the other hand, you think "I do
not like opera because my musical taste is undeveloped,
but nevertheless I will attend the best operas until I gradually develop that taste," that is a splendid policy.

Honesty is the first step in self-development.

Intelligence

Intelligence is the glory of God. Put it into every corner of your life.

He worked hard and hoarded money all his life. He got no happiness out of it for himself or for others. Then he died—and as he could not take it with him, someone else had the congenial task of spending it. *Unintelligent.*

She walked ten blocks in bad weather to save a nickel, wore out a dime's worth of shoe leather, got a cold, and was in bad humor for three days. *Unintelligent.*

He took the greatest care of his car and used only the best gasoline, although he could always buy a new car, but he neglected his body, ate too much food and all the wrong things, and got no real exercise and no proper rest, until he wrecked his health. *Unintelligent.*

She wanted to be popular and have lots of friends, but she had a bad tongue and was known to be critical and gossipy, so that gradually but surely she became completely isolated. *Unintelligent.*

He was ambitious and wanted to be an executive some day, but meanwhile he did as little work as he could, was sulky when an extra job came along, and was often late or missing from his place. Then he was surprised and hurt because the promotions always went to someone else. *Unintelligent.*

The examination was going to mean a lot to him, but he neglected steady preparation, wasted his time on unimportant activities, and was at a late party the night before. Tired and unprepared, he naturally failed. *Unintelligent.*

176

He was always polite and helpful to strangers. In fact his outside manners were perfect, but he was boorish and self-centered at home with the ones whom he really loved. *Unintelligent.*

He worked and worried over a thousand unimportant passing things and neglected the development of his soul. *Unintelligent.*

Stop Limiting God

T he principal reason why prayers are not answered, why treatments do not demonstrate, is because in our hearts we limit the power of God. The Bible constantly tells us that the people got into trouble because *they limited the Holy One.*

When you say, "There is no way out of my difficulty," what can it possibly mean except that *you* cannot see a way out? When you say, "It is too late now," what can that possibly mean except that it is too late for *you?* When you say, "This problem is too great," what can it possibly mean, except that it is too great for the faith that *you* have at the moment?

When you pray or treat you are turning to the power of God and surely you will admit that God is omnipotent, and therefore nothing can be too difficult, or too late, or to soon for *Him.* You will surely admit that Infinite Wisdom knows at least more than you do, to put the thing rather mildly. Well, Infinite Wisdom takes action when we pray and so our own limitations do not matter—unless we think they do.

Children often find themselves completely overcome by a difficulty that a grown-up person easily solves. What to the child seemed an impossibility is quite easy to his father, and so even our greatest difficulties are utterly simple to God. Think of a child just learning subtraction. He reaches the point where he understands how to take six from eight. Then he gets the little problem of taking eight from twelve and his faith in arithmetic collapses. To him it is obvious that you cannot take eight from two and that is the end of the matter. Teacher, however, sees a little farther and shows him how it can easily be done.

Infinite Wisdom knows a simple way out of every difficulty, a simple answer to every problem, a beautiful and joyous solution to any dilemma that can come to anyone, and it is only our ingrained habit of limiting God that keeps Him from giving us perfect harmony. Do not limit the power of God for good in your life.

It Was Long Since Proved—

*T*hat the secret of life is to cooperate with Nature instead of fighting her.

That bodily health is the greatest of all blessings.

That if you have no confidence in yourself, you are licked before you start.

That those who rely upon bluff or deceit do not last, because honesty really is the best policy.

That intelligent planning and lots of hard work are a necessary part of any achievement.

That a mental attitude of forgiveness and toleration makes for health, happiness, and all-round success.

That you often overlook the choicest things in life because they are so easy to obtain—the sunrise and the sunset, the starry host on a clear night, the taste of fresh clean air, the sight and smell of flowers and trees, and the fresh rain on your face.

Treat the "Because"

When you find yourself thinking that your prayer cannot be answered for any reason whatever—treat that reason. When something says to you that you cannot demonstrate "because"—treat the *because*.

When you think, I cannot demonstrate because I have not enough understanding—treat for understanding. When you think, I cannot treat because I have a headache—treat the headache. When you think, I cannot demonstrate because I am full of doubts—treat the doubts. When you think I cannot demonstrate because it is now too late—treat against the time illusion. When you think, I cannot demonstrate in this part of the country—treat against the space illusion. When you think, I cannot demonstrate this thing because of my age—treat your age belief. When you think, I cannot demonstrate because someone else will hinder me—treat the belief in a power other than God.

No matter what name the *because* may give itself, it is still your belief in limitation. Be loyal to God and know that He and He alone has all power.

Treat the *because*.

Make It Subconscious

Before an idea can work in our lives it must be accepted by the subconscious mind. When the idea *is* accepted by the subconscious it *must* work in our lives. Knowledge that is only in the conscious (or fore-conscious) mind can have no practical effect. It is when it is accepted in the deeper layers that it becomes dynamic.

Physicians know consciously what perfect anatomy and hygiene would be, but they are not healthier than any other class because this knowledge is not in the deeper layers of their minds. If it were, they would demonstrate perfect health. We students of metaphysics know that God is Love and Intelligence and we believe it, but it is not until that idea is accepted in the deeper levels of our subconscious that we shall have perfect peace of mind and the all-round harmony that comes with it.

From the scientific point of view then, our problem is to get the ideas we wish to demonstrate accepted by the subconscious. Then the rest will follow.

Shepherd Not Bell Hop

W hen you feel a desire to improve yourself or your conditions, it means that
God has inspired you with that splen-
did idea, and He who inspired you with the idea will give
you the power to carry it out.

This means that when we are praying for health, harmony, and true prosperity, we are obeying God by that
very act—not beseeching Him to grant it; much less ordering Him to do so.

Some people talk as though Divine Mind were there
to take our orders, but, of course, this is absurd. It is we
who obey the orders of Divine Mind. God's orders to us
take the form of inspirations and aspirations for better
things.

The Bible says, "The Lord is my shepherd." Some foolish people seem to think it says, "The Lord is my bell
hop." They talk about *ordering what you want,* and probably they are guilty of nothing worse than very confused
thinking.

We do not order God. He inspires us, but He does not
compel us to accept his inspirations if we do not wish
to. We have free will to be negative or positive, constructive or destructive, as we choose. But always the path upward will be in obedience to God and to the laws of His
universe.

Is It a Lie?

Thoughtless people sometimes say that our affirmations and meditations are foolish because we state what is not so. "To claim that my body is well or being healed when it is not, is only to tell a lie," said one distinguished man some years ago.

This is to misunderstand the whole principle. We affirm the harmony that we seek in order to provide the subconscious with a blueprint of the work to be done. When you decide to build a house, you purchase a vacant piece of ground, and then your architect prepares drawings of a complete house. Actually, of course, there is no such house on the lot today, but you would not think of saying that the architect was drawing a lie. He is drawing what is to be, in order that it may be. So, we build in thought the conditions that will later come into manifestation on the physical plane.

To wait like Mr. Micawber for things to "turn up" is foolish, because you will probably die before they do so. What is your intelligence for if not to be used in building the kind of life that you want? Very primitive men in prehistoric times rejoiced when they found food growing anywhere, and then they waited, perhaps for years, until they happened to find another crop. Today we use our intelligence and plant in good time the actual crops that we want and the amount that we consider necessary. We do not sit about hoping that wheat or barley may fortunately come up somewhere. If we did that, civilization would collapse.

The time has come when intelligent men and women must understand the laws of Mind, plant consciously the crops that they desire, and just as carefully pull up the weeds that they do not want.

The Means Is Not the End

The object of treatment is to produce a certain state of mind. That state of mind constitutes a true understanding concerning the problem in question and freedom from fear in connection with it. When this state of mind is attained, the demonstration must and does follow.

Whatever produces the required state of mind is a good treatment. Repeating certain affirmations, reading certain verses in the Bible, using the "Presence Card" or the "Golden Key," or any other "method" of producing that state of mind is a good treatment.

Note, however, that using the affirmations or reading spiritual literature is not an end in itself. It is the uplifted state of mind that is the end. Many sincere Christians have come to mistake the means for the end and think that praying mechanically or going through certain forms constitutes the spiritual life, but this is not so. The spiritual life is the search for higher states of consciousness and nothing else.

Whether you are praying to heal a problem (physical or otherwise) or for the general development of your soul, the higher level of understanding is the objective.

M. Y. O. B.

Mind your own business. One of the first rules on the spiritual path is that you must attend strictly to your own business and not interfere with that of others. Your neighbor's life is sacred and you have no right to try to manage it for him. Let him alone. God has given him free will and self-determination, so why should you interfere?

Many well meaning people are constantly "butting in" to their neighbors' lives without invitation. They pretend to themselves that their only desire is to help, but this is self-deception. It is really a desire to interfere.

Interference always does more harm than good. Actually those who mind other people's business always neglect their own. The man who wants to put your house in order has always made a failure of his own life. *M. Y. O. B.*

Of course, this does not mean that you are not to help people whenever you can; in fact, you should make it a rule to try to do at least one kind act every day; but you must do it without interfering or encroaching. When in doubt, claim Divine Guidance.

It is always right to give your neighbor the right thought. Under any circumstances it can only do good to "Golden Key" him when you think of him.

Don't fuss—*God is running the universe.*

Divine Wisdom Works in You . . .

 f you do not use a hundred units of energy to do five units of work—or try to kill flies with a steam hammer.

If you do not cross bridges before you come to them.

If you do not allow yourself to be disorganized by trifling occurrences that you know perfectly well are of no importance.

If you realize that it is more economical to spend money wisely than to hoard it.

If you understand that what you have to live with is your own concept of things.

If you keep your personal business to yourself.

If you really practice the motto, *live and let live.*

Circulation

T he law of circulation is a Cosmic Law. That means that it is true everywhere and on all planes.

The law is that constant rhythmical movement is necessary to health and harmony. Now the opposite of circulation is *congestion*, and it may be said that all sickness, inharmony, or trouble of any kind is really due to some form of *congestion*.

If you think this subject out for yourself you will be fascinated to find how generally true it is and in what unexpected places it appears.

Much ill health is due to emotional *congestion*. This leads to *congestion* of the nerve, blood, and lymphatic fluids, producing disease.

The depression belief under which the country labored for ten years was a case of congestion. There was plenty of raw material, machinery, and skill, and a very widespread demand for goods, but a case of *congestion* occurred!

The dust bowl trouble and its allied misfortune, the floods, is, of course, an example of *congestion*.

War itself is really due to frustrated circulation on many planes of existence.

Some students of metaphysics shut their minds to the reception of new truth, and this always produces mental *congestion* and a failure to demonstrate.

You should treat yourself two or three times a week for free circulation on all planes—by claiming that God is bringing this about.

Are You a Fetish Worshiper?

The lowest form of idolatry (if one form of idolatry can be said to be lower than another) is fetish worship. The most degraded savages in Africa are those most addicted to the worship of fetishes. Unfortunately there are many "civilized" savages in Europe and America suffering from the same weakness. Fetish worship is by no means extinct even among earnest church-goers, even among sincere metaphysical students.

To give power to any material object is to make a fetish of it, and to worship that fetish, and to that extent to be a savage. Fetish worship is a denial of the power of Divine Spirit and, in plain English, it is the sin of idolatry forbidden by the First Commandment.

Last year a man came to me in great distress. I knew him as an earnest and successful student of metaphysics. Five or six years ago he opened a small restaurant in New York and has made a great success of it. He began business during the worst days of the depression belief, when shops were failing all around him. This café had changed hands two or three times in the previous two years, ruining each successive proprietor. By regular daily spiritual treatment this man had built the business into a success and was making a larger income than he ever made in the so-called days of prosperity. Then something happened. He had saved the first dollar bill he took in when he opened the place, framed it and hung it on the wall behind the counter "for luck!" It hung there four or five years. Then one week-end last fall he had the whole place cleaned out, painted, and refurnished.

For forty-eight hours gangs of men came and went, and during the proceedings the dollar bill disappeared.

The poor man was almost hysterical with fear. He said, "My luck is gone. I would pay a thousand dollars to get that bill back"—and he was a student of metaphysics!!

Of course I scolded him soundly, told him he had made a fetish and was worshiping it and that this was the time to get free. He got free, and the business continues to flourish.

A woman came to me in the same state of mind. She had been very happily married for ten years, and now she had lost her wedding ring; she had left it on a public wash basin. She said, "This may mean that our marriage will go wrong." I said, "Your marriage has been successful because you have loved and trusted one another, not because of a metal ring. Buy another ring at the nearest shop and be sensible."

Even the Bible itself can be made a fetish. I have known people who said they would not like to be without a Bible in the house, and yet they never opened it.

See if you are worshiping any fetishes, and if so, get rid of them, and worship God.

Have You Ever Noticed . . .

*T*hat God gave you two eyes and two ears but only one tongue?

That an animal never eats when it is sick, and that domestic animals keep themselves fit and well by exercise, stretching, and relaxing?

That a bad workman quarrels with his tools and that the grumbler is never efficient at his job?

That when a place is kept scrupulously clean, everything else is likely to be right too?

That the cemeteries are full of people who thought they couldn't afford to take a rest, or didn't have the time?

That Americans travel thousands of miles and spend thousands of dollars to rave over foreign scenery, when there is probably something just as beautiful within a hundred miles of home?

That almost anything on earth that is worth having can be obtained in New York City?

Have you ever noticed?

Have You Seen the Leopard?

T he circus came to town for one evening and little Johnny's father took him to see it. His cousin in New York had written him a glowing report of the show, especially of a big spotty leopard in a cage. His mother, his aunt, his uncle, and his big sister all gave him dimes to spend; he got a whip, and a flag, and a cowboy hat, and popcorn, and lemonade.

They sat close to the ring, and he saw everything that happened in the big top, and then they went outside, and father took him into all the side shows and right down the alley where the animals were.

When they left the circus he was so tired he could hardly keep his eyes open. Father remarked, "Well, you certainly had a good time," and the child replied, "Yes, Daddy, but I didn't see the leopard." When they arrived home, Mother said, "Did you see all the great big elephants?" and he replied, "Yes, Mama, but I didn't see the leopard." Uncle inquired, "Did you like that wonderful trapeze performance high up in the air?" He replied, "Yes, uncle, I did, but I didn't see the leopard." Sister said, "Weren't the little midgets cute?" And he replied, "Yes, they were, but I didn't see the leopard." Auntie said, "Didn't you love all those beautiful horses galloping around and those clever people standing on their backs?" He replied, "Yes, auntie, I loved it, but I didn't see the leopard."

Some people pass through the world like little Johnny at the circus. They get many good things out of life, but there is some particular thing that they really want, and yet they manage to miss it. They put off getting it or doing it, or they let unimportant obstacles stand in the way. Then when the end of the road comes, in spite of all that life has given them, *they haven't seen the leopard.*

The businessman who always wanted to make a flower garden himself but never got around to it; the woman who always wanted to see the Rocky Mountains, or the Pyramids, or Fujiyama, and had money to go, but did not like to spend it; the person who always wanted to be able to speak French, but never had time to take a lesson— these people all went to the circus but failed to see the leopard.

Stop wasting time and money for things that you do not really want and go out and get the things that you do want. A real wish—something that you know is not either wrong or manifestly foolish—comes from God, and God will open the way if you let Him. There really is not much use in seeing the whole circus if you do not see the leopard.

Keep on the Beam

Today most commercial flying is done on a radio beam. A directional beam is produced to guide the pilot to his destination, and as long as he keeps on this beam he knows that he is safe, even if he cannot see around him for fog or get his bearings in any other way.

As soon as he gets off the beam in any direction he is in danger, and he immediately tries to get back onto the beam once more.

Those who believe in the Allness of God, have a spiritual beam upon which to navigate on the voyage of life. As long as you have peace of mind and some sense of the Presence of God, you are on the beam, and you are safe, even if outer things seem to be confused or even very dark, but as soon as you get off the beam you are in danger.

You are off the beam the moment you are *angry* or *resentful* or *jealous* or *frightened* or *depressed,* and when such a condition arises you should immediately get back on the beam by turning quietly to God in thought, claiming His Presence, claiming that His Love and Intelligence are with you and that the promises in the Bible are true today. If you do this you are back on the beam, even if outer conditions and your own feelings do not change immediately. You are back on the beam and you will reach port in safety.

Keep on the beam and nothing shall by any means hurt you.

Grant Always Fought

N ever recognize evil as having any reality. Never grant it the courtesy of the slightest or most formal acquiescence. Even though you may not be able to demonstrate over error for the time being, still you must not recognize it as having any power or reality.

Every time you speak or think of evil as having any power—you give it that much power. Every time you allow it to scare you—you give it that much authority.

Always fight error in thought—not in the sense of struggling with it, but fight it in the sense of knowing that it is only false belief. Do not let it rest quietly in thought, but harass it.

An old soldier who was with Grant during most of the Civil War once said:

"The difference between Grant and McClellan was this—McClellan was a mighty fine soldier, knew all the military textbooks by heart and what you ought to do—but he wouldn't fight. When Lincoln would ask him to fight, he would say, 'Not ready yet' or 'We must be thoroughly prepared for a thing like that; next year maybe.' But Grant, he was always fighting. No matter how few men Grant had with him, if the enemy was anywhere near, Grant took a sock at him. Grant would always fight."

The only attitude for the metaphysical student is: "I believe in Divine Harmony and nothing else. I do not believe there is any power in evil, and it is not going to get any recognition from me. The Truth about my problem is true now, not next week or next year but *now*, and the

Truth concerning anything is all that there is of it." This is the scientific way of fighting and harassing error—to see that it has no chance to dig itself in. This is the General Grant touch.

Judge not according to the appearance, but judge righteous judgment.

The Lost Corot

There is a quaint old legend that is firmly believed in the artists' colony in Paris. It appears that many years ago a poor struggling artist was so hard up that he did not have even enough money to buy a piece of canvas upon which to paint what he felt sure would be a masterpiece.

Going along the quays he saw an old daub selling third hand for a few sous, frame included. It was supposed to represent Napoleon III in full dress uniform, and doubtless had proudly adorned the wall of some cottage in the days of the Second Empire. The artist decided that he could clean off the picture and use the canvas for his own work.

Arrived home, he proceeded to remove Napoleon III, a task that gave him no trouble, and to his astonishment found that there was another picture underneath. The last artist had not even taken the trouble to remove the original but simply worked over it.

When the last traces of Napoleon III had disappeared, he was amazed to discover what looked to him like a very fine Corot. He promptly submitted his find to the experts. It was pronounced a genuine and very fine Corot, and, of course, his days of poverty were ended.

Whether this story is truth or fable, it is a perfect allegory of the nature of man as we know him. Outside we find the "marred image" showing limitation, sin, sickness, and inharmony—the unskillful daub; but underneath is the master work of the Great Artist, and our prayers and treatment act by clearing away the false accretions—the "many inventions" of the carnal mind—that the already existing Truth and Harmony may appear.

What a Shame!

eard an amusing story the other day, and it happens to be also a great metaphysical parable.

A man was sitting in a train when he noticed that his neighbor was muttering and grumbling under his breath in a very angry manner.

He said, "What's the trouble?"

His neighbor replied, "I've been disgracefully treated, but I'll get even."

Our friend inquired, "What happened?"

The stranger replied, "It was a dream I had last night."

"A dream?" repeated the astonished inquirer.

"Yes, I dreamt I was going up Fifth Avenue, New York, and I picked up a wallet containing a thousand dollars. It had the name and address of the owner inside, and, being an honest man, I took it to him immediately. It was up in the Bronx, and I had a twelve mile journey and spent a nickel for my subway fare. And what do you think he did? Thanked me and handed me a quarter."

"He did?"

"Yes, a thousand dollars—the money was in bills and I could easily have kept it if I hadn't been honest. And he hands me a quarter! It makes me mad that I didn't kick him."

Before his astonished hearer could murmur, "But it was only a dream," the train stopped at a station, and the angry stranger disappeared, still muttering vengeance.

For students of metaphysics, comment would be superfluous. For others, suffice it to say that to worry over the griefs of yesterday, to allow negative things in the past to spoil the perfection of today, is just as foolish as to be angry over the annoyances of a dream.

You Have a Divine Agency

S ome students of metaphysics are fond of referring to themselves as "channels," channels of Spirit, channels of Divine Will, and so forth. The idea is quite correct, but I am not sure that the word is well chosen. To me a channel seems to be rather a hollow thing. To be a channel does not seem interesting or inspiring. I prefer to think of man as the *agent* of God, for that is what he is.

A Western Union boy, for example, could be well called a channel, in that sense, because he conveys a message from one person to another, but he doesn't know what the message is, and, of course, has no interest in it, and no responsibility; a telephone operator could also be thought of as a channel between the two subscribers whom she connects. Compare these positions with the *agent* of, say, a business firm. The head office is, let us suppose, in Chicago. The firm sends an agent to Denver to transact its business there, perhaps to open a branch office or store. He represents the firm. He transacts its business—well or ill. If he is industrious and wise, he makes a great success; if he is stupid or lazy, he fails, and the firm gets no business in that town. He is responsible, he has discretion, and such an *agency* has an absorbing interest to the right man.

Or, a government sends an agent to a foreign country, where he represents the home government, negotiates all kinds of important arrangements, and, according to his management of the business, advances or retards the cause of those who sent him.

You are the agent of God at the place where you find yourself. You have reason, intuition, free will, and self-determination, and you can be a good and efficient agent, a poor agent, or a positive detriment, according to the way in which you conduct your life.

To be an agent of God is the most wonderful destiny that you could ever dream of. Practice His Presence in all that you do and you will indeed be His agent and the living witness to the glory of His Name.

Have You Lost Your Wigwam?

During the old days in the West, a party of trappers entered a clearing in the forest and found themselves face to face with an Indian who was obviously lost. The leader said, "Indian lost?"

The Noble Red Man drew himself proudly up to his full height and replied, "No!! Indian not lost. Indian here. Wigwam lost."

Nevertheless he was lost, even though he would not admit it.

When things go wrong with us it is because for the time being we are lost. We have lost contact with the Divine Center of our being, and this loss of contact produces fear (conscious or subconscious), and this fear must break out as inharmony in some phase of our lives.

As a rule, people do not like to admit that they have drifted away from what they know to be the Truth. They prefer to pretend that somehow it is Divine Harmony that has slipped away from them. "I am not lost," is their thought, "I am here. I am not at fault; it is outer conditions that are reacting upon me." Nevertheless, it is they who are lost, and until they re-establish their Divine Contact and know the Truth about the inharmony, they cannot find themselves again. They are fooling themselves, like the Indian. *Outer conditions are never cause but always effect.*

When something goes wrong you must survey the situation with as little emotion as possible. Then remind yourself of what you know to be the Divine Truth behind the appearance. Then cleave to this, through thick and thin, and it is only a matter of time before you will see harmony re-established for all concerned.

The realization of Divine Truth must heal any condition in time.

I Wonder Why . . .

Many people are bored in a world full of so many thrillingly interesting things.

People who brag the most usually have the least to offer, and people who promise the most are usually those who perform the least.

Human beings cannot arrange to live together in peace—seeing that we have to stay on the same globe and there is no way of getting off.

We are all so conscious of faults and failings in ourselves, and yet we expect the other fellow to be perfect.

Middle-aged people always think that if they could start life over again they would make no mistakes, and yet they do not always act very wisely in the present.

People read so many dull, trashy books and magazines, and forget the most vitally interesting book of all—the Bible.

People waste their lives and energies on a thousand useless, tiresome things, and neglect the only thing that really matters—finding God.

I wonder why!

How to Get a Demonstration

Here is one way of solving a problem by Scientific Prayer, or, as we say in metaphysics, of getting a demonstration.

Get by yourself and be quiet for a few moments. This is very important. Do not strain to think rightly or to find the right thought, and so forth, but just be quiet. Remind yourself that the Bible says *Be still, and know that I am God.*

Then begin to think about God. Remind yourself of some of the things that you know about Him—that He is present everywhere, that He has all power, that He knows you and loves you and cares for you, and so forth. Read a few verses of the Bible or a paragraph from any spiritual book that helps you.

During this stage it is important not to think about your problem, but *to give your attention to God.* In other words, do not try to solve your problem directly (which would be using will power) but rather become interested in thinking of the Nature of God.

Then claim the thing that you need—a healing or some particular good that you lack. Claim it quietly and confidently; as you would ask for something to which you are entitled.

Then give thanks for the accomplished fact; as you would if somebody handed you a gift. Jesus said, "When you pray believe that you receive and you shall receive."*

Do not discuss your treatment with anyone.

Try not to be tense or hurried. *Tension and hurry delay the demonstration.* You know that if you try to unlock a

*Matthew 21:22.

door hurriedly, the key is apt to stick, whereas, if you do it slowly, it seldom does. If the key sticks, the thing is to stop pressing, take your breath, and release it gently. To push hard with will power can only jam the lock completely. So it is with all mental working.

In quietness and confidence shall be your strength.

No Depression in Nature

T he majority of the American people have been suffering under a belief in depression for a number of years and are only now drawing out of it. It has been a belief only, because *there has been no depression in nature.*

This is the real tragedy, that people have suffered want in the midst of plenty. The United States is by far the richest country in the world. It contains, *now,* everything that we could possibly want to furnish every man, woman, and child in the country with a good living. There are more minerals in the ground than we can possibly use. Our factories are filled with the finest machinery in the world. We have no lack of highly trained technicians and skilled workmen. We have all the labor that we need. All kinds of raw material are available. We have enormous tracts of the most fertile soil on the globe. In fact, there is nothing that mankind could possibly desire that is not available to the American people *now.*

If Almighty God Himself were to say to us, "What are you waiting for? What do you want that I have not provided you with?" we would be obliged to answer, "Nothing."

If anyone thinks that gold is necessary, the answer is that we already have the greater part of the gold supply of the world, right here, and far more than we ever had in our history before.

So it is obvious that the depression is purely mental and is absolutely nothing but fear. *Nature knows nothing of depression,* and if we would but rid ourselves of irrational fear, we need not know it either.

I believe that every unemployed man and woman could be at remunerative work in thirty days; every mill and factory working full time; every store doing capacity business; and every farmer making a good living; if the people would shake off the spell of fear.

Those who understand Scientific Prayer can help to end depression very rapidly if each will know the Spiritual Truth for the whole country in general, and for his own business in particular, every day.

The Great Adventure*

W hen you are in difficulties, look upon the overcoming of them as a great adventure. Resist the temptation to be tragic, to give way to self-pity or discouragement, and approach the problems as though you were an explorer seeking a path through Darkest Africa, or an Edison working to overcome difficulties in connection with a new invention.

You know that there is a way out of any difficulty whatever, no matter what it may be, through the changing of your own consciousness by prayer. You know that by thus raising your consciousness any conceivable form of good that you can desire will be yours, and you know that nobody else can by any means hinder you from doing this when you really want to do it—relatives, customers, employers, the government, bad times, so-called—nothing can hinder you from the rebuilding of your own consciousness, and this rebuilding is the Great Adventure.

*From the chapter, "Getting Results by Prayer," in *Power Through Constructive Thinking*.

Problems and Opportunities

T hanksgiving day, this year, finds us at a point in world history where, upon the threshold of the New Age, we are confronted by major problems of every kind. I think I cannot do better than quote here what I wrote in the pamphlet, *The Historical Destiny of the United States:*

"Now, does all this mean that I think that the future history of the United States is going to be a simple and easy path of uninterrupted development? No, I do not suppose anything of the kind. The fact is, that a quiet and uneventful life is rather the mark of age and decrepitude than of youth and vigor. It is the destiny of youth to have great problems and great difficulties to tackle and to solve, and it is the glory of youth to have the vision and the energy to do both without fear. When the life of a man or of a nation becomes gentle and uneventful, it means that its work is done, but the work of this nation is only beginning, and I expect, therefore, that in the years ahead of us there will be great problems and difficulties and even dangers to be met and overcome. But I know that as long as the American people are true to themselves, and to the American Dream—as long, that is to say, as they remain united in essentials—so long will they continue to remain undefeated, and so long will they fulfill their destiny of service to the world. Difficulties and problems are good things in themselves because every difficulty overcome is proof of a further advance in consciousness."

The American Spirit*

The finest Constitution and the greatest Declaration of Independence ever made are but phrases until they are incorporated into the practical lives of living people. And so, unless you are seeking to embody the American Spirit in your own personal life and conduct, you are no true American, even though you may have authentic Mayflower ancestry.

If you allow yourself to judge the worth of a man by anything except his character, if you discriminate against him for any reason that is outside of his own control, you are no true American. If you judge him by his parents, or his connections, or his external conditions, instead of by himself, you are no true American. If you allow yourself to be hampered by any question of precedents or traditions, you are no true American. If you think that any kind of honest work can be degrading, or what is called *infra dig.*, you are no true American. If you would not rather be independent in plain surroundings than dependent in luxury, you are no true American. If you allow yourself to be dazzled by any exalted office, or intimidated or hypnotized by pretentious titles or gorgeous uniforms of any kind, you are no true American. And, unless you believe that the poorest boy or girl doing chores around the farm, or playing on the sidewalk of a great city, is just as likely—given the opportunity—to turn out to be the greatest soul in the nation as the child who is reared in the lap of luxury, then you are no true American.

*From the pamphlet, *The Historical Destiny of the United States.*

The American Constitution*

The American Constitution then, would be unworkable unless the people were self-reliant, self-determined, and resourceful. There are nations who do not care for these things and do not possess them. I suppose we all have our favorite virtues. My own are self-reliance, initiative, resourcefulness, courage. I like these things better than anything else, but there are people who do not, and there are nations that do not. There are nations, for example, whose people like to be directed and ordered about, who like to be led everywhere and told what to do and where and when to do it. Such people can do great things in the world through mass action, but they could not work such a constitution as ours. This Constitution calls for people who prefer to take care of themselves. It is intended for the kind of men and women who desire to manage their own lives, take their own risks, fend for themselves, and be personally independent—and these very things are just the outstanding characteristics of the majority of American people.

But notice that, among other things, this policy means that there is sure to be a certain amount of suffering, because, when we are free we always make some mistakes. A convict in prison has very little chance to make mistakes. He is told when to get up and when to go to bed, is given his food and obliged to eat it. He is told what clothes to wear, what work to do, and how he is to

*From the pamphlet, *The American Spirit*.

do it. He is taken out into a yard for exercise, and when it is thought he has had enough exercise he is taken back. He can hardly go wrong, he can hardly make a mistake, but neither, of course, does he ever learn anything. A free man will make mistakes, and he will learn by them. He will suffer, but suffering is worthwhile when you learn something. When you are not free you cannot learn, and so the suffering is only wasted.

Note very particularly that the Constitution does not guarantee equality of lot. You cannot have equality of lot because human nature varies. No two men have the same character. No two men have quite the same amount of ability. Again, some will have less talent but a strong character and go to the top for that reason. Other men—we all know some of them—have great talents, but character is lacking, so they remain at the bottom. This being so, there cannot be equality of lot, but there can be, and there is in America, true equality, which is *equality of opportunity.*

The City on a Hill*

*Ye are the light of the world. A city that is set on an hill
cannot be hid.*

—MATTHEW 5:14

The state of your soul is always expressed in your outer conditions and in the intangible influence that you radiate at large. There is a Cosmic Law that nothing can permanently deny its own nature. Emerson said: "What you are shouts so loudly that I cannot hear what you say." In the Bible, the "city" always stands for consciousness, and the "hill," or "mountain," always means prayer or spiritual activity. "I will lift up mine eyes unto the hills from whence cometh my help." "Except the Lord keep the city, the watchman waketh but in vain." The soul that is built upon prayer cannot be hidden, it shines out brightly through the life that it lives. It speaks for itself, but in utter silence, and does much of its best work unconsciously. Its mere presence heals and blesses all around it without special effort.

Never try to force other people to accept Spiritual Truth. Instead, see to it that they are so favorably impressed by your own life and conduct, and by the peace and joy that radiate from you, that they will come running to you of their own accord, begging you to give them the wonderful thing that you have. "I (the Christ Truth) if I be lifted up, will draw all men unto me." To do this is to make your soul truly the *city upon a hill that cannot be hidden* because it is the Golden City, the City of God.

*From *The Sermon on the Mount.*

216

The Supreme Right*

I n the long run, no one can retain what does not belong to him by right of consciousness, nor be deprived of that which is truly his by the same supreme title.

Therefore, you will do well not to lay up to yourself treasures upon earth, but rather to lay up treasure in heaven; that is, the understanding of Spiritual Law. If you are looking to outer, passing, mutable things for either happiness or security, you are not putting God first. If you are putting God first in your life, you will not find yourself laboring under undue anxiety about anything, for *where your treasure is, there will your heart be also.*

*From *The Sermon on the Mount.*

The Great Hippodrome Meeting*

T he success of the meeting at the Hippodrome on 14 March* exceeded all expectations. Long before ten o'clock, a crowd of people filled the sidewalk for the whole block and down 44th Street, and by the time the service started over six thousand people were crammed into the huge auditorium. People sat on the steps and around the gangways, and the lobbies were also filled, these having been provided with loudspeakers.

It was undoubtedly the greatest meeting that has ever been held in the Truth movement, and it is a wonderful proof of the eager desire that people have today for a demonstrable religion that is purely spiritual.

One of the striking features of the service was the wonderful character of the meditation. The vast audience maintained perfect silence for four minutes without any sense of strain or effort, contemplating the thought: *The Christ of God is reborn in me today with great power.*

In the sermon it was stressed that the second coming of the Christ is the coming of this Truth to the general public in this age as never before. Hitherto, throughout the ages, individuals and small groups have understood the Allness and Availability of God, but now for the first time the mass of mankind is to receive it. This is the heralding of a new age of individual demonstration. In consequence of this revolutionary change in

*(Sunday, 14 March 1937.)

218

thought in the people's minds, all sorts of natural, political, and social upheavals will be seen for a few years, but as the new understanding begins to work out, an era of great peace, harmony, and unprecedented progress will dawn for humanity.

"Genuine-Life Prayer Meeting Attracts Earnest Thousands"*

"Somebody said the other day that when you see a crowd leaving a public building, you can guess what sort of meeting it has been—whether a gospel meeting or a prize fight, a circus or a classical concert—but that nobody could place the crowd that comes from the Manhattan Opera House every Wednesday night, because it contains every kind of person.

"As a matter of fact, it is a cross-section of New York's population at prayer meeting, the regular Wednesday evening meeting of the Church of the Hearing Christ, when the pastor, Dr. Emmet Fox, explains the life of man from the angle of psychology and metaphysics.

"Here in this streamlined setting the ever well-known Wednesday night prayer meeting catches up with life, as it were. And every week, rain or shine, over 4,000 New Yorkers make their way, in skyscraper fashion, to this replenishing station for faith, in the opera house.

"That the church chooses to present its message in this candid camera manner is not illogical in this modern day and age. But if walls have ears, as the proverb says, they must ring with amazement as the magic wand is waved within these four, and they are tuned, week after week, from swing music to prayer.

*Reprinted from the *New York World Telegram*, Saturday, 30 October 1937.

"Dr. Fox has found, he says, that the real need people have—the one thing for which they should really wish—is sufficient knowledge of their own mentality to enable them to meet every problem and wish as it arises day by day. He believes that there is a solution to every problem and that prayer can find it.

"*Prayer does change things,* is his vital message, and you must conduct the affairs of your soul in a businesslike way if profitable and harmonious results are to be forthcoming. It is prayer that opens the door of the soul so that the Divine Power may work its will. *Miracles can and do happen as the result of prayer.*"

Show Me Thy Face!*

Show me Thy face—one transient gleam
Of loveliness divine,
And I shall never think or dream
Of other love than Thine;
All other light will darken quite,
All lower glories wane,
The beautiful of earth will scarce
Seem beautiful again.

Show me Thy face—I shall forget
The weary days of yore;
The fretting thoughts of vain regret
Shall hurt my soul no more;
All doubts and fears for future years
In quiet trust subside,
And naught but blest content and calm
Within my breast reside.

Show me Thy face—the heaviest cross
Will then seem light to bear;
There will be gain in every loss
And peace with every care.
With such light feet the years will fleet,
Life seem as brief as blest;
Till I have laid my burden down
And entered into rest.
—PSALM 102:1, 2

*This poem is a wonderful treatment. The author is unknown.